At Issue

Should Religious Symbols Be Allowed on Public Land?

Other Books in the At Issue Series:

Are Americans Overmedicated?

Are Newspapers Becoming Extinct?

Are Social Networking Sites Harmful?

Casualties of War

Cell Phones and Driving

Concealed Weapons

Food Safety

Green Cities

How Can the Poor Be Helped?

Human Embryo Experimentation

Is Organic Food Better?

Is Socialism Harmful?

Media Bias

Sexting

Should Junk Food Be Sold in Schools?

Should Juveniles Be Given Life Without Parole?

Should There Be an International Climate Treaty?

At Issue

Should Religious Symbols Be Allowed on Public Land?

Louise I. Gerdes, Book Editor

GREENHAVEN PRESS
A part of Gale, Cengage Learning

Detroit • New York • San Francisco • New Haven, Conn • Waterville, Maine • London

Christine Nasso, *Publisher*
Elizabeth Des Chenes, *Managing Editor*

For more information, contact:
Greenhaven Press
27500 Drake Rd.
Farmington Hills, MI 48331-3535
Or you can visit our Internet site at gale.cengage.com

Articles in Greenhaven Press anthologies are often edited for length to meet page requirements. In addition, original titles of these works are changed to clearly present the main thesis and to explicitly indicate the author's opinion. Every effort is made to ensure that Greenhaven Press accurately reflects the original intent of the authors. Every effort has been made to trace the owners of copyrighted material.

LIBRARY OF CONGRESS CATALOGING-IN-PUBLICATION DATA

Should religious symbols be allowed on public land? / Louise I. Gerdes, book editor.
p. cm. -- (At issue)
Includes bibliographical references and index.
ISBN 978-0-7377-5167-3 (hardcover) -- ISBN 978-0-7377-5168-0 (pbk.)
1. Religious observances on public property--Law and legislation--United States. 2. Christian art and symbolism--Law and legislation--United States. I. Gerdes, Louise I., 1953-
KF4868.R45S54 2011
342.7308'52--dc22

2011000941

Printed in the United States of America

1 2 3 4 5 15 14 13 12 11

ED136

Contents

Introduction 7

1. The Controversy over Religious Symbols on Public Land: An Overview 13
Thomas J. Billitteri

2. The Founders Did Not Intend to Forbid Religious Symbols on Public Land 18
Michael Gaynor

3. If Public Space Is Open to One Religion, It Must Be Open to All 27
Charles C. Haynes

4. Seeking to Remove Religious Symbols from Civic Life Is Impossible 31
Gregory Rodriguez

5. Removing Religious Symbols from Public Land Distorts the Christian Past 35
Michael Medved

6. No Clear Test Exists for Religious Symbols and the Establishment Clause 40
Avern L. Cohn and Bryan J. Anderson

7. The Establishment Clause Does Not Ban Religious Symbols on Public Land 54
Ted Cruz and Kelly Shackelford

8. The Establishment Clause Should Not Be Used to Alter Historic Memorials 58
Michael Sean Winters

9. War Memorial Crosses Dishonor Veterans of Other Faiths 62
Sandhya Bathija

10. War Memorial Crosses Symbolize Courage and Patriotism, Not Religion **71**
Patrick Brady

11. War Memorial Crosses Symbolize Christianity and Endorse Religion **74**
Geoffrey R. Stone

12. Radical Secularist Attacks on Monument Crosses Threaten Religious Freedom **78**
Newt Gingrich

13. Bad Reasoning of Activist Judges Allows Religious Symbols on Public Land **81**
Bob Ritter

14. The Courts Struggle over When to Allow Religious Symbols on Public Land **86**
Ira C. Lupu, David Masci, and Robert W. Tuttle

15. Promoting Religious Displays on Public Land Can Dampen Holidays **99**
Sandhya Bathija

Organizations to Contact **109**

Bibliography **115**

Index **120**

Introduction

The First Amendment to the US Constitution, one of ten amendments known as the Bill of Rights, states, in part, "Congress shall make no law respecting an establishment of religion, or prohibiting the free exercise thereof." The first clause, known as the establishment clause, limits government promotion of religion, and the second, known as the free exercise clause, limits the government's power to interfere with the free expression of religious belief. The tension between these two clauses is central to the debate over whether religious symbols should be allowed on public land. Two core questions create the tension between these two clauses. The first question is whether a religious symbol on public land constitutes government establishment of religion or whether it is instead the free expression of religious beliefs. The second question is, if the latter is true, does the religious symbol, by expressing one religious belief, therefore suppress the beliefs of others, having the effect of establishing a particular religion.

The decisions state and local governments have made in an effort to effectively answer these seemingly circular questions have led to confusion and rancor, particularly during the December holiday season. Unsure whether a nativity scene standing alone in the public square violates the First Amendment, some states allow all religions to participate rather than ban religious displays altogether. The public response varies from amusement to claims by the Christian right that governments have declared a war on Christmas. This annual, nationwide public debate reflects the true heart of the conflict—a culture war that centers around another question, whether the United States is a Christian nation. While some claim that those who wrote and signed the US Constitution and the Bill of Rights intended the United States to be a Christian nation, others argue that the Founders meant to build a wall of separation between church and state. The US Supreme Court is the final arbiter of constitutional questions. Unfortunately, the Court's decisions concerning religious symbols on public land, including annual holiday displays, have led to further confusion. Commentators on both sides of the debate look to US history and the rhetoric of the Founders to support their views. Thus, consideration of this historical rhetoric is useful to understand the conflict.

Those who believe it is appropriate to have Christian symbols on public land cite evidence that the Founders intended the United States to be a Christian nation. According to retired US Army Reserve Chaplain E. Ray Moore Jr., "The indisputable historic fact is that America's culture, laws and civil institutions were founded on Christian principles."[1] Indeed, he adds, most of the nation's Founders professed to be Christians. Moore and like-minded commentators often cite the 1892 case *The Church of the Holy Trinity v. United States*, in which Supreme Court Justice David J. Brewer declared, "This is a Christian nation." In his opinion, Brewer claimed the Founders intended that the American people had the right to promote the Christian religion without interference from the government. The First Amendment, Brewer reasoned, was meant to block the federal government from becoming involved with religion. Based on Brewer's reasoning, Moore concludes, "The 'wall of separation' concept meant keeping the federal government out of the church, not keeping Christian values out of government."[2]

On the other side of the debate, those who oppose religious symbols on public land argue that the Founders did not intend the United States to be a Christian nation and, in fact, intended to create a high wall of separation between church and state. Reverend Barry W. Lynn, executive director of Americans United for Separation of Church and State, asserts,

1. E. Ray Moore Jr., "Is the United States a Christian Nation? Yes," *CQ Researcher*, January 15, 2010.
2. Ibid.

"There is absolutely no historical evidence for the view that we were formed as a Christian nation, and there's vast evidence to the contrary."[3] He and like-minded scholars often cite the 1797 Treaty of Tripoli. The Treaty was negotiated by George Washington, signed by John Adams, and ratified, unanimously, by the Senate. The Treaty states, "The government of the United States is not in any sense founded on the Christian religion."[4] These analysts do not dispute that the United States was founded when the culture was primarily Christian. Nevertheless, maintains John Fea, associate professor of American history, "I don't think the evidence is there to suggest [the United States was founded] as a uniquely Christian nation. Most of the Constitution does not mention God at all, and when it does it talks about religious freedom or the Establishment Clause. So to suggest that in some way [the Founders] were trying to create a republic that somehow uniquely privileged Christianity is simply ahistorical."[5]

Those on both sides of the debate over religious symbols on public land also cite historic US Supreme Court opinions to buttress their views. Clashes over the interpretation of the Bill of Rights began soon after the passage of the 14th Amendment, which applied the Bill of Rights to the states. However, in the early years following the ratification of the 14th Amendment, Supreme Court decisions focused on economic and corporate issues, not on issues involving religion or civil rights and liberties. Not until the years following World War II, when the role of religion in civil society became elevated by cultural and political trends, did battles over the meaning of the First Amendment's establishment and free expression clauses begin in earnest.

In *Everson v. Board of Education* (1947), the Supreme Court upheld a New Jersey law that allowed a local school board to

3. "Government and Religion," *CQ Researcher*, January 15, 2010.
4. "Treaty of Peace and Friendship," 1796. Text available at http://avalon.law.yale.edu/18th_century/bar1796.asp.
5. "Government and Religion," *CQ Researcher*, January 15, 2010.

reimburse parents for the cost of sending their children to public or private schools, including religious ones, on public buses. In support of the view that the establishment clause erected a high barrier between church and state, Justice Hugo Black called upon the words of one of the nation's Founders, Thomas Jefferson. "In the words of Jefferson," he wrote, "the clause against establishment of religion by law was intended to erect 'a wall of separation between church and state.'" Black added, "That wall must be kept high and impregnable. We could not approve the slightest breach." Those who oppose religious symbols in public spaces often call upon Jefferson's "wall of separation." Indeed, Jefferson's words are "as familiar in today's political and judicial circles as the lyrics of a hit tune,"[6] claims James Hutson, chief of the Library of Congress Manuscript Division.

Despite Black's fervent words in *Everson*, when it comes to decisions on the constitutionality of religious symbols on public land, the Supreme Court has, in the eyes of some commentators, created more confusion than clarification. Thus, those hoping to support their views with enlightening words from the Supreme Court often have been disappointed. The Court's contrasting decisions about public displays of the Ten Commandments are reflective of the challenges analysts face. In two 5-4 rulings, the Court came to different conclusions. In *Van Orden v. Perry* (2005), the Supreme Court argued that a large, decades-old Ten Commandments monument on the grounds of the Texas capital did not violate the establishment clause. However, in *McCreary County v. American Civil Liberties Union of Kentucky* (2005), the court argued that displays of the Ten Commandments at two Kentucky courthouses did violate the clause.

Observers on both sides came to different conclusions about the impact of these cases. "To the extent that the deci-

6. James Hutson, "'A Wall of Separation,'" *Library of Congress Information Bulletin*, June 1998.

sions provided guidelines for the further cases that are all but certain to follow," *New York Times* journalist Linda Greenhouse suggests, "it appeared to be that religious symbols that have been on display for many years, with little controversy, are likely to be upheld, while newer displays intended to advance a modern religious agenda will be met with suspicion and disfavor by the court."[7] Some think the implication of these cases is more significant. These commentators claim that conservative forces within the court may in fact support displays that favor religion generally. In an interview with *Hamodia*, a Jewish newspaper, Supreme Court Justice Antonin Scalia suggests, "It has not been our American constitutional tradition, nor our social or legal tradition, to exclude religion from the public sphere."[8] In Scalia's view, Supreme Court decisions that argue that the establishment clause requires neutrality regarding religion have misinterpreted the clause. Religious neutrality, he argues, "is not the American tradition."[9]

Despite Scalia's claims of a religious American tradition, the nation's religious landscape is changing. Although 65 percent of Americans polled in 2007 believe the Founders intended the United States to be a Christian nation, the number of Americans who profess to be Christian is shrinking. Indeed, only 76 percent identified themselves as Christian in 2008, 10 percent fewer than in 1990, and 15 percent claimed no religious preference. Moreover, Supreme Court cases concerning the establishment and free exercise clauses have been narrowly decided, often in 5-4 decisions. Thus, how these clauses should be applied to cases concerning religious symbols on public land remains hotly contested in the Supreme Court and in the court of public opinion. The controversy is

7. Linda Greenhouse, "Justices Allow a Commandments Display, Bar Others," *New York Times*, June 28, 2005.
8. Y.M. Lichtenstein and T. Moskovits, 'Justice Scalia: 'The American People Respect Religion,'" *Hamodia*, September 16, 2009.
9. Ibid.

far from over as the divergent viewpoints in *At Issue: Should Religious Symbols Be Allowed on Public Land?* make clear.

1

The Controversy over Religious Symbols on Public Land: An Overview

Thomas J. Billitteri

Thomas J. Billitteri, a public policy journalist from Fairfield, Pennsylvania, is a staff writer for CQ Researcher, *a publication that conducts in-depth analysis on current issues.*

While most Americans are not offended when religious displays such as nativity scenes, menorahs, or other religious symbols appear on public land, in the courts the issue is extremely contentious. While some US Supreme Court justices believe that such displays violate the US Constitution's Establishment Clause, which prohibits government establishment of religion, others believe that such displays are appropriate. Still other justices argue that religious displays are unconstitutional only when they convey the message that the government endorses a particular religion. With little guidance, outcomes in the lower courts are unpredictable. Some activists argue that religious symbols on public land convey the message that the government endorses that religion while others counter that the Constitution guarantees religious freedom, not freedom from religion. The controversy continues as new religious display concerns reach the courts.

Despite the Constitution's prohibition against government "establishment of religion," most Americans don't seem bothered when crèches, menorahs and other such religious

Thomas J. Billitteri, "Government and Religion," *CQ Researcher*, vol. 20, no. 2, January 15, 2010, pp. 25–48. Reprinted by permission.

symbols appear on public property. A 2008 Rasmussen poll found that 74 percent of adults thought such displays should be allowed. The Pew Research Center has found similar popular support.

A Conflicted History in the Courts

Yet, the presence of religious symbols on government property has a long and sometimes conflicted history in the courts.

In 1980 the Supreme Court ruled that a Kentucky law requiring public schools to post a copy of the Ten Commandments in all classrooms was a violation of the Establishment Clause. But in 1984, the court said it was constitutional for a Nativity scene to be displayed in a Rhode Island town square.

"Since these two decisions in the 1980s, the Supreme Court and lower federal courts have issued somewhat unpredictable rulings, approving some religious displays while ordering others to be removed," the Pew Forum on Religion & Public Life noted in a 2007 review of religious display cases. . . .

The presence of religious symbols on government property has a long and sometimes conflicted history in the courts.

Added Pew, "[t]he lack of clear guidelines reflects deep divisions within the Supreme Court itself. Some justices are committed to strict church-state separation and tend to rule that any government-sponsored religious display violates the Establishment Clause. These same justices also believe that, in some circumstances, the Establishment Clause may forbid private citizens from placing religious displays on public property." But "[o]ther members of the court read the Establishment Clause far more narrowly, arguing that it leaves ample room for religion in the public square." Meanwhile, other justices have taken a middle path, arguing that "a religious display placed in a public space violates the Establishment Clause only when it conveys the message that the government is endorsing a religious truth."

A Range of Views

Some activists firmly oppose religious displays. Lynn of Americans United for Separation of Church and State, for example, argues that "a bright-line rule would make sense: If it's a government-sponsored event, icon or symbol, it should not be religious. When you put up a manger scene at Christmas and it's the government that owns it, it looks like the government is endorsing that religion," he argues.

Hooper, the Council on American-Islamic Relations spokesman, takes a broader view, arguing that "as long as everyone has equal access" to a site, "we're not opposed to it."

"It's really up to each religious community to make sure it has equal access," he adds. "We've dealt with this in the past as an organization. If a local library has a Christmas display, we don't ask people to go and tell them to take down the Christmas display. We say, 'Look, reserve it for the next time Ramadan comes along.' It's in our court, really."

Some activists firmly oppose religious displays.

Carey of the National Association of Evangelicals says that while the group is "not overly concerned about most of these issues," many cases concerning religious displays "do raise constitutional issues and need to be carefully studied on their merits.

"So much depends on context," says Carey, "There's a difference between 'In God We Trust' on our money or having a Nativity scene at city hall. You look at the context in the community."

Freedom of or Freedom from Religion?

What's needed is a "common sense" approach to the issue of religious displays, Carey argues. "We don't want the government to be in the position of establishing or favoring a particular religion." Many displays don't do much to do that, Carey says, "but if something were endorsing and furthering a particular religion, we would not be in favor of that."

In the crèche conflict in Chambersburg, Pa., the Nativity scene had been displayed for years in the town's Memorial Square, and some residents believe that's where it should have remained. "Jesus is the reason for the season," resident Kelly Spinner told a local media outlet. "They're taking that reminder away from us. I don't think it's fair. What's next? Santa Claus? A Christmas tree?"

The council president, Bill McLaughlin, argued that Chambersburg was "a victim of the tyranny of the minority," adding that "the Constitution guarantees 'freedom of religion'" but says nothing about "freedom from religion."

But a local Jewish resident noted that council members let him put a "Seasons Greetings" sign incorporating religious symbols from a variety of backgrounds on the town square in 1996. "You really can't pick and choose what goes up there," he said. "Once you let one group in, whether it's Christians, Jews, Muslims, then you have to let other groups in also."

Lynn, commenting broadly on the issue of religious displays and not the Chambersburg flap, says that "if you truly say 'this courthouse lawn is open to everybody'—if you're really willing to do that—that I think the Constitution does permit, but I think that's a dopey idea." In places that have opened public spaces to displays of all persuasion, he says, "you get a cluttered lawn. People trip over stuff on their way to pay their parking tickets."

Avoiding State Entanglement with Religion

Among the most contentious religious-display issues in recent years has been the placement of religious mottoes on automobile license plates. The Indiana legislature approved state-issued plates bearing the motto "In God We Trust" in 2006, and Florida followed suit in 2008.

In November, a federal judge ruled that South Carolina couldn't issue plates showing the image of a cross in front of a stained-glass window and bearing the words "I believe." U.S. District Judge Cameron Currie said a law approving the plates amounted to a "state endorsement not only of religion in general, but of a specific sect in particular."

Lt. Gov. André Bauer, who had advocated the bill approving the plates, called the ruling "another attack on Christianity" and said Currie was a "liberal judge appointed by [President] Bill Clinton."

But Currie ruled correctly in an "absolutely clear-cut" case," said Thomas Crocker, an assistant professor at the University of South Carolina Law School. Her decision was "not out to denigrate religion, but it's out of a historical understanding that problems for both politics and religion can flow from the state's entanglement with religious practices." . . .

2

The Founders Did Not Intend to Forbid Religious Symbols on Public Land

Michael Gaynor

Michael Gaynor, an attorney who writes on political and religious issues, is a regular contributor to Renew America, a Christian organization that promotes issues of moral conservatism.

The American Civil Liberties Union and activist judges who oppose placing religious symbols on public land have misinterpreted the intent of the nation's founders. The Framers, those who framed the US Constitution, never intended the Establishment Clause to prohibit the government from recognizing God or to require that it promote religious neutrality. Jefferson's oft-misinterpreted statement that there be a "wall of separation between church and state" meant the clause would keep government from interfering with religious freedom. The statement was not meant to prohibit the government from acknowledging God. Thus, placing a cross on a public waterway to memorialize victims of Hurricane Katrina does not constitute the establishment of religion. Indeed, the Framers would have found this interpretation absurd.

The American Civil Liberties Union's [ACLU] sinister secular extremist presumption is getting even worse. Now the ACLU wants to stop a cross from being placed on private property, at private expense, in Louisiana, in honor of Hurri-

Michael Gaynor, "ACLU (Anti-Cross Leftists United) Strikes Again!" Renew America, August 9, 2006. Reprinted by permission.

cane Katrina victims. The significance of this overreach should be immense. If publicized, it should inspire most voters to support presidents and United States senators who will nominate and confirm strict constructionists instead of judicial activists[1] to all federal courts (especially the United States Supreme Court). Justices like Chief Justice John Roberts and Associate Justice Samuel A. Alito, Jr., appointed by President [George W.] Bush, NOT Justices like Ruth Bader Ginsburg and Stephen Breyer, appointed by former President [Bill] Clinton.

A Despicable Development

Karen Turni Bazile reported this despicable development in *The Times-Picayune*, a New Orleans newspaper, fittingly, on a Sunday, August 6, 2006, in this article titled "Katrina memorial bears Jesus' face":

> "Alarmed by newspaper reports that a hurricane memorial in St. Bernard Parish will feature a cross bearing a likeness of the face of Jesus, the American Civil Liberties Union of Louisiana is reminding parish officials of the Constitution's separation of church and state.
>
> "Never one to back down, Parish President Henry 'Junior' Rodriguez has a simple reply: 'They can kiss my ass.'
>
> "In a July 28 letter to Rodriguez and other officials, Louisiana ACLU Executive Director Joe Cook said that the government promotion of a patently religious symbol on a public waterway is a violation of the Constitution's First Amendment, which prohibits government from advancing a religion.

1. Strict constructionist judges avoid drawing inferences based on the presumption that once the court has established a clear meaning of the law, particularly the US Constitution, no further investigation is required. Strict constructionist legal philosophy has come to mean legal conservatism. In the view of strict constructionists, judicial activists exceed their power by making law rather than interpreting it, thereby influencing public policy through their decisions.

"Rodriguez did not say whether he has responded to Cook's letter, but in an interview, he said he sees nothing improper about the memorial, which will be mounted near the shoreline of the Mississippi River-Gulf Outlet at Shell Beach. The cross and accompanying monument listing the names of the 129 parish residents who died in Hurricane Katrina are earmarked for what the parish says is private land and are being financed with donations, Rodriguez said.

"Nonetheless, Cook asked the parish to erect a religiously neutral symbol and also voiced concern that the Parish Council was sanctioning a religious monument.

"Returning Rodriguez's volley, Cook added, 'It would be better if he would kiss the Constitution and honor it and honor the First Amendment.' . . .

"As for the parish's statements that the memorial is being done outside government's auspices, Cook seems unconvinced.

"While the ACLU thinks a memorial to the storm and its victims is 'clearly appropriate,' Cook said, St. Bernard's is 'still all very questionable. I think there is official government involvement with the endorsement and advancement of this clearly religious symbol.'"

A Monumental Misconstruction

As usual, the ACLU is relying on a monumental misconstruction of the First Amendment's Establishment Clause to nullify the religion liberty guaranteed by the First Amendment's Free Exercise of Religion Clause. The United States Constitution does NOT require complete separation of church and state, or compel the United States government and state governments to be strictly neutral as between religion and "irreligion," or prevent the United States government and state governments from acknowledging God and supporting religion generally.

The contrary ACLU claim is a secular extremist myth that needs to be exploded. It perverts the Establishment Clause to please the secular extremists, by ignoring history.

In the mid nineteenth century, secular extremists of that time challenged (unsuccessfully) the constitutionality of the military chaplaincy.

The United States Constitution does NOT . . . prevent the United States government and state governments from acknowledging God and supporting religion generally.

After careful study, the Senate Judiciary Committee issued a report explaining the establishment clause: "The clause speaks of 'an establishment of religion.' What is meant by that expression? It referred, without doubt, to the establishment which existed in the mother country, its meaning is to be ascertained by ascertaining what that establishment was. It was the connection with the state of a particular religious society, by its endowment, at public expense, in exclusion of, or in preference to, any other, by giving to its members exclusive political rights, and by compelling the attendance of those who rejected its communion upon its worship, or religious observances. These three particulars constituted that union of church and state of which our ancestors were so justly jealous, and against which they so wisely and carefully provided. . . ."

The report further stated that the Founders were "utterly opposed to any constraint upon the rights of conscience" and therefore they opposed the establishment of a religion in the same manner that the church of England was established. But, the Founders "had no fear or jealousy of religion itself, nor did they wish to see us an irreligious people. . . . They did not intend to spread over all the public authorities and the whole public action of the nation the dead and revolting spectacle of 'atheistic apathy.' Not so had the battles of the revolution been fought, and the deliberations of the revolutionary Congress conducted."

A similar House Judiciary Committee report explained that "an establishment of religion" was a term of art with a specific meaning:

The Founders 'had no fear or jealousy of religion itself, nor did they wish to see us an irreligious people.'

"What is an establishment of religion? It must have a creed, defining what a man must believe; it must have rights and ordinances, which believers must observe; it must have ministers of defined qualifications, to teach the doctrines and administer the rites; it must have tests for the submissive, and penalties for the nonconformist. There never was an establishment of religion without all these."

Memorial crosses obviously do NOT constitute an establishment of religion as that term was used in the First Amendment. And the Free Exercise Clause authorizes the placement of a cross on private property, at private expense.

Disregarding History

BUT, in 1947, in *Everson v. Board of Education*, the United States Supreme Court disregarded history and misconstrued the Constitution at the urging of a tiny secular extremist minority and the expense of the overwhelming religious majority in ruling that neither federal nor state governments "can pass laws which aid . . . all religions. . . ."

In so ruling, the Court presumptuously substituted its personal view for the views of those who founded the United States, wrote and ratified the Articles of Confederation and the Constitution, and adopted the First Amendment and misused a much-quoted letter in which Thomas Jefferson had described the First Amendment as "building a wall of separation between church and state."

Justice Antonin Scalia, in a footnote to his compelling dissent in *McCreary County v. American Civil Liberties Union of Kentucky* (2005), the infamous Kentucky Ten Commandments case, not only lamented the insidious effect of *Everson*, but exposed and lambasted it as specious and the "evidence" on which it purportedly was based as "a bill of goods": "The fountainhead of this jurisprudence, *Everson v. Board of Ed. of Ewing*, based its dictum that '[n]either a state nor the Federal Government . . . can pass laws which . . . aid all religions,' on a review of historical evidence that focused on the debate leading up to the passage of the Virginia Bill for Religious Liberty. A prominent commentator of the time remarked (after a thorough review of the evidence himself) that it appeared the Court had been 'sold . . . a bill of goods.'"

[Thomas] Jefferson did not envision that the institutional separation he had in mind would ever be expanded to prohibit the United States from making reasonable accommodations to religion.

In misinterpreting the Establishment Clause, the United States Supreme Court misused a statement by Jefferson in an 1802 letter to a Baptist group that "the whole American people . . . declared that their legislature should make no law respecting an establishment of religion, or prohibit the free exercise thereof, thus building a wall of separation between church and state." Jefferson's much quoted statement was misinterpreted as a prohibition against government acknowledging God and supporting religion generally instead of only a protection of churches from governmental interference. The "wall of separation" that Jefferson contemplated was a wall that keeps government from interfering with religious freedom, not a wall that keeps any religious expression out of schools, courthouses and other public places. Jefferson's own preamble to the Virginia Statute of Religious Freedom explicitly acknowledged "Almighty God" as "the Holy Author of our religion" and "Lord both of body and mind."

Jefferson did not envision that the institutional separation he had in mind would ever be expanded to prohibit the United States from making reasonable accommodations to religion and recognizing God on its currency, in its courts or in its classrooms. Jefferson's own actions as President demonstrate that his words were misinterpreted. As President, Jefferson attended voluntary and nondiscriminatory religious services held at the Capitol (as did President Madison). In 1803, Jefferson called on Congress to approve a treaty with the Kaskaskia Indians that provided for the United States to pay a Catholic missionary priest $100 a year. It was not an oversight. Jefferson later recommended two other Indian treaties with similar provisions. Jefferson also extended three times a pre-Constitution act that had designated lands "[f]or the sole use of Christian Indians and the Moravian Brethren missionaries for civilizing the Indians and promoting Christianity." If the United States Supreme Court was right, then Jefferson himself repeatedly violated the establishment clause. But, as the House Judiciary Committee report set forth in detail, "an establishment of religion" requires much more.

The Founders Favor Neutrality

The First Amendment did not create a wall between church and state. It prohibited Congress from making a law "respecting an establishment of religion, or prohibiting the free exercise thereof."

The kind of separation that was intended is suggested by Pierre L'Enfant's plan for a national cathedral. In 1791, Congress selected the site to be the capital of the United States. George Washington, previously President of the Constitutional

Convention and then President of the United States, then commissioned L'Enfant to design an overall plan for the future seat of government. That plan included a church "intended for national purposes, such as public prayer, thanksgiving, funeral orations, etc., and assigned to the special use of no particular Sect of denomination, but equally open to all." The Founders and Framers favored governmental neutrality among denominations, but they never expected government to be barred from supporting religion generally to please a tiny Godless minority.

Traditional nonsectarian acknowledgments of God by federal or state government, including the inclusion of "under God" in the Pledge of Allegiance and "In God We Trust" on United States currency, the recitation of a voluntary nondenominational prayer in a public school, and the display of a Ten Commandments monument in both federal and state courthouses, were intended to be constitutionally permissible, and coercive or sectarian governmental acts that establish a religion or prohibit or penalize the free exercise of religion (or personal choice NOT to be religious) were intended to be unconstitutional.

The Founders and Framers favored governmental neutrality among denominations, but they never expected government to be barred from supporting religion generally to please a tiny Godless minority.

The notion that a cross (with or without a depiction of Jesus) could not constitutionally be erected on private property at private expense would have struck Americans as absurd up until 1947, when the United States Supreme Court arbitrarily extended the First Amendment's establishment clause, by judicial invention, to separate church and state in a way that inhibits the free exercise of religion required by the First Amendment's Free Exercise Clause but provides freedom from religion to the unreligious minority. THAT surely was not contemplated by the men who drafted and ratified the Constitution and the First Amendment, and would not have been comprehensible to them.

America was not conceived of by those men as a theocracy or a secular state, but as "one nation, under God." The notion that under the Constitution the United States government cannot acknowledge God and instead must maintain a strict neutrality between religion and irreligion and crosses could not be erected on private property at private expense would have been considered absurd by virtually all the Founders, Framers, members of the First Congress and members of the state legislatures that ratified the First Amendment.

3

If Public Space Is Open to One Religion, It Must Be Open to All

Charles C. Haynes

Charles C. Haynes, director of the Religious Freedom Education Project, writes and speaks extensively on religious liberty and religion in American public life. He has been the principal organizer and drafter of consensus guidelines on religious liberty in schools. Haynes is the author or co-author of six books, including First Freedoms: A Documentary History of First Amendment Rights in America *and* Religion in American Public Life. *He also chairs the Committee on Religious Liberty of the National Council of Churches.*

Despite efforts by Thomas Jefferson and James Madison to disestablish religion from government in the Bill of Rights, activists continue to fight to erect Christian symbols on government land while opposing the freedom of other religions to do the same. If the government allows one religion to place a religious display in public space, then it must open the space to all beliefs. The outrage by believers at displays placed on public land by non-believers emphasizes that the United States has not achieved true religious freedom. At the same time, non-believers do not advance their cause by erecting displays that denigrate religious faith.

Charles C. Haynes, "Even in December, a Right for One Remains a Right for All," First Amendment Center, December 21, 2008. Reprinted by permission.

Just when I thought the Christmas wars couldn't get more ridiculous or hostile, along comes the uproar over dueling holiday displays in the rotunda of Washington's state Capitol.

First a holiday tree, then a menorah, followed by a crèche—and now a "winter solstice" placard declaring all of the above to be hokum.

The red-and-green solstice sign, placed by the Freedom From Religion Foundation, describes religion as "myth and superstition that hardens hearts and enslaves minds." Happy holidays to you, too.

Addressing the Outrage

The in-your-face display proved too much for the hundreds of Washingtonians who rallied to protest the state's decision to give the anti-religion group space alongside the Nativity. After TV commentator Bill O'Reilly, the self-appointed defender of all things Christmas, weighed in, the brouhaha went national.

O'Reilly is outraged—outraged! He calls Washington Gov. Christine Gregoire a "weak and confused leader" who supports "political correctness gone wild."

But truth be told, Bill, the governor has no choice under the First Amendment. Of course, the state of Washington could have kept all displays out of the rotunda. Or the state might have been able to put up some official holiday display in the Capitol—as long as the overall message wasn't an endorsement of religion. But that's not what happened.

Instead, some years ago the state allowed a business group to put up the "holiday tree" as part of a charity drive. Then in 2006, a rabbi asked to put up a menorah, followed by a Christian group demanding the right to put up a crèche. Rather than go to court, state officials granted space to all three.

Opening Up Government Space

Hence the current December dilemma: If the state opens up government space to one private group to proclaim its message, it can't turn around and prohibit others.

For its part, the Freedom From Religion Foundation, which describes itself as an association of freethinkers (atheists and agnostics), claims it doesn't want any holiday displays in state capitols.

"But if the state is going to permit a nativity display and create a public forum," says a spokesman for the group, "then we want to be sure that the views of the 16% of the U.S. population who is not religious are also represented."

If the state opens up government space to one private group to proclaim its message, it can't turn around and prohibit others.

Now other enterprising citizens want in on the holiday fun. One fellow has requested space for a "Festivus" pole, celebrating a fictional holiday created on the sitcom "Seinfeld." Someone else wants a display honoring the Flying Spaghetti Monster.

Most bizarre of all, Fred Phelps and members of his Westboro Baptist Church of Topeka, Kan.—the anti-gay group infamous for protesting at military funerals—wants to erect a sign with a ditty called "Santa Claus Will Take You to Hell" (sung to the tune of "Santa Claus is Coming to Town"). Only in America.

Last week, overwhelmed state officials finally declared a "moratorium" on any new displays until they can review their policy. Good luck with that in court.

Not Just a West Coast Phenomenon

Lest you think all of this silliness is a kooky West Coast phenomenon: After a private group put up a crèche in the Illinois state Capitol this month [December 2008], the freethinkers followed with their aforementioned winter-solstice sign. Conflict is sure to follow in Illinois and in other states foolhardy enough to open up their capitols' rotundas.

If culture warriors have their way, competing holiday displays are likely to proliferate. A nationwide movement to erect Nativity scenes on government property is gaining steam—and the freethinkers, Fred Phelps and the spaghetti monster are sure to follow close behind.

I'll confess it's hard for me to understand why some religious groups insist on using government property to proclaim their messages, especially when crèches are omnipresent in front of homes, churches and other private property. And I can't grasp why freethinkers think they advance their cause by denigrating religious faith.

But under the First Amendment, when government space is open to one, it is open to all. Like it or not, the days of a religious monopoly in government settings are numbered.

Thomas Jefferson and James Madison, you may recall, attempted to end the monopoly more than 200 years ago by disestablishing religion in Virginia and then pushing for "no establishment" in the Bill of Rights.

Under the First Amendment, when government space is open to one, it is open to all.

But despite legal disestablishment, the religious-freedom playing field has been far from level in America. That explains the anger of many non-believers who feel that government often treats them as second-class citizens by privileging religion.

The free-for-all in Washington may look like a circus. But it's also a healthy reminder that religious freedom isn't only for the religious—nor is free speech just for the polite.

4

Seeking to Remove Religious Symbols from Civic Life Is Impossible

Gregory Rodriguez

Gregory Rodriguez, a regular columnist for the Los Angeles Times, *is a scholar and director of the California Fellows Program at the New America Foundation, a public policy institute. He writes on issues of national identity, social cohesion, assimilation, race relations, religion, immigration, ethnicity, demographics, and social and political trends in publications such as* The New York Times, The Wall Street Journal, *and* The Economist.

Religion and culture have become so entangled that it would be impossible, if not narrow-minded, to separate them. Some religious symbols have become so generalized that they have secular as well as religious significance. The Star of David, for example, is not only a symbol of Judaism but also has ethnic and political significance. Although the US government should not endorse any particular religion, efforts to separate religion from government are unrealistic. In fact, the ideal of religious freedom has roots in the religious convictions of early Americans. Indeed, many of the religious symbols activists hope to ban from the public sphere are part of America's culture and history.

I'm all for the separation of church and state. I believe that government endorsement of any particular religious sect or tradition has a corrosive effect on both the state and the faith

Gregory Rodriguez, "The Many Meanings of a Cross," *Los Angeles Times*, October 19, 2009. Reprinted by permission.

in question. But I also think the attempt to separate religion from government is veering toward a foolish, parochial and ultimately impossible quest to separate religion from culture.

Last week, the ACLU of Southern California's Peter Eliasberg argued the case of *Salazar vs. Buono* before the U.S. Supreme Court. The case, which involves a cross that has stood, in various forms, for 75 years as a memorial to World War I veterans in the Mojave Desert, elicited a heated exchange between Eliasberg and Justice Antonin Scalia.

In a debate over whether the cross, which is on property surrounded by the Mojave National Preserve, violates the 1st Amendment ban on the establishment of religion, Eliasberg argued that a cross "is the predominant symbol of Christianity" that "signifies that Jesus is the son of God and died to redeem mankind from our sins." Therefore, it shouldn't be allowed to "stand alone" as a war memorial in a national park. Scalia offered a different definition. "The cross is the most common symbol of the resting place of the dead," he said. The *Times* reported that Scalia "sharply disagreed" with Eliasberg.

Eliasberg responded: "I have been in Jewish cemeteries. There is never a cross on a tombstone of a Jew," he said.

Scalia wasn't persuaded: "I don't think you can leap from that to the conclusion that the only war dead that the cross honors are the Christian war dead. I think that's an outrageous conclusion."

I see Eliasberg's point, but Scalia's notion that the cross has become a generalized symbol of memorial strikes me as true too. Sure, you might suspect that Scalia, a practicing Roman Catholic and a well-known conservative, is simply seeking an argument that would allow the cross in this case to pass constitutional muster, but he's also accurately pointing to how entangled religion and culture are.

Eliasberg's reading that the cross has a specialized religious significance symbolizing the son of God who died for mankind's sins seems way too narrow an interpretation. Does it mean that? Yes. Does it have other significance? Absolutely.

Consider another common symbol, the Star of David. It is a symbol of Judaism, but it is also an ethnic, national and political symbol. It'd be hard, then, to say that its significance is entirely spiritual or theological.

Sometimes, religious symbols have historical significance that in some contexts can transcend their theological meaning. Five years ago, under threat of a lawsuit by the ACLU, the Los Angeles County Board of Supervisors voted to remove a cross from the county seal. In the iconography of the seal, which had a number of symbolic images on it, the cross stood for the Catholic missions whose founding in the late 18th century signaled the dawn of modern Los Angeles history. But the ACLU claimed it represented "an impermissible endorsement of Christianity by the county government." The supervisors didn't fight it, but they should have.

Religion is at the core of American identity. To seek to root it out of civic life and culture altogether is not only impossible, it's silly.

In his 1996 book, "The Truth of Broken Symbols," philosopher and theologian Robert C. Neville observed that in predominantly secular societies, religious symbols often lose their theological specificity and become broadly generalized. In fact, he points to the American military cemetery in Cambridge, England, where a "sign explains that a Star of David on a tombstone signifies the grave of a Jewish soldier whereas a cross signifies 'all others.'" Likewise, he notes that "clergy blessing governmental ceremonies are performatively invoking divine aid by their very presence but are likely to pray in terms so general as not to be specific to their own religion's symbol system."

Culture is moving toward greater syncretism, something you can see in the increase in interracial marriage and the election of a black president. As for religion, a recent survey found that Americans who don't identify with any religion—now 15% overall and 22% of all adults ages 18 to 29—make up the fastest-growing religious "tradition" in the country.

The problem with the ACLU's approach to religious symbols is that it's zero sum and old school—it is, dare I say it, puritanical. Its narrow vision could rob the public sphere of symbols we need to understand who we are, what we're about and where we came from.

The truth is that even as we become a more secular country, religion will continue to be an integral part of our society, history and culture. Indeed, our very notions of politics and good government are the legacy of zealously religious people. Even our ideals of religious freedom and church/state division have roots in the theological convictions of Colonial and Revolutionary-era Baptists and Presbyterians as much as in the Enlightenment. Even if we don't as a nation profess one faith or another, religion is at the core of American identity. To seek to root it out of civic life and culture altogether is not only impossible, it's silly.

5

Removing Religious Symbols from Public Land Distorts the Christian Past

Michael Medved

Michael Medved is an American radio host, author, conservative political commentator, and film critic who hosts a nationally syndicated talk show. He writes a regular column for USA Today *and is the author of* The 10 Big Lies About America: Combating Destructive Distortions About Our Nation.

The goal of efforts by radical secularists to remove Christian symbols from America's public spaces is to eradicate the nation's Christian past, not to protect Americans from the establishment of a national religion. War memorial crosses are meant to honor fallen American warriors who have made the ultimate sacrifice. Indeed, a majority of these soldiers were Christian. Such memorials pose no threat to the nation's non-Christian population. What is at risk is the eradication from memory of the fact that Christian ideals motivated many historical movements in the United States, including the battle to free slaves and resist international communism.

An attack on religious symbolism has been waged for several years now on a barren hilltop in California. A simple cross to honor fallen soldiers is simply too much for militant 'separationists,' who seem intent on disassembling this country's Christian past.

Michael Medved, "A War on Memory," *USA Today*, June 18, 2007. Reprinted by permission.

What shocking visual image inspires so much fear, disgust and outrage that even in this era of unfettered free expression, federal courts feel compelled to take drastic steps to cover it up?

Judges will rarely use their power to hide public sculptures depicting sadistic brutality, or to obscure billboards peddling sex and nudity, but in the California desert they've ordered the concealment of a simple white cross that has honored the nation's war dead for more than 70 years.

In 1934, the Veterans of Foreign Wars erected a monument on a barren hilltop known as "Sunrise Rock" in the Mojave National Preserve to commemorate "the dead of all wars." More than a half-century later, the American Civil Liberties Union of Southern California challenged the memorial, claiming that it violated the Establishment Clause of the First Amendment because the cross (recognized by the government as a war memorial) stood on public land. The 9th Circuit Court of Appeals ordered the dismantling of the monument, but Congress took action in 2004 to authorize the transfer of the ground surrounding the cross to private parties.

A federal district judge invalidated that transaction, even as officials responsible for the desert refuge took steps to hide the cross while the legal wrangling continued. Government agents covered the offending crossbeam with boards, making it look like a crude screen, or a shallow box, perched incongruously on a stick in the middle of the California desert.

An Easy, Favorite Target

The absurd status of this ongoing struggle shouldn't obscure its serious and alarming undercurrents—including a common attitude among militant "separationists" that treats Christian symbols with more hostility and less tolerance than those of any other religious tradition.

Imagine that the U.S. Holocaust Memorial Museum decided for some reason to erect a large Star of David on top of its stark building in Washington. Would the ACLU object to the raising of this religious (and, yes, national) symbol on a structure that has been built, after all, on federal land? In the unlikely event that anyone stood up to oppose such symbolism, reasonable people would respond that the Jewish star represented an appropriate commemoration to the millions of predominantly Jewish victims honored by the museum.

My Jewish kids . . . would be damaged by enforced ignorance of the Christian ideals and idealists behind crucial historical movements—from the pilgrims to the civil rights marchers.

By that logic, a cross (whether in the Mojave Desert or in another controversial war memorial on the top of Mount Soledad near San Diego) represents a similarly suitable tribute to fallen warriors who have died for the United States—because the overwhelming majority of those soldiers considered themselves Christians. To this day, more than 85% of Americans describe themselves as Christians, and many recent studies (including the excellent *Imperial Grunts* by Robert D. Kaplan) report that devout Christian believers are, if anything, overrepresented in our volunteer Army.

The government recently authorized a Wiccan symbol (a five-pointed star, or pentacle) to appear on the military cemetery gravestone of a GI who died in Afghanistan—despite objections by some Christian activists that Wicca (a proudly pagan tradition that incorporates elements of druidical nature worship) carries unwholesome associations with witchcraft and Satanism. The armed forces rightly gave the family of the fallen soldier the right to choose its own symbolism in tribute to him, even if that symbol appeared on public property. After all, the military already allows grave site recognition of Buddhism, Hinduism, Islam, Mormonism and even atheism (represented by a stylized diagram of an atom).

In the same sense that no one should feel offended by honoring the war dead with symbols of their faiths, so, too, even the most radical secularists ought to accept the war memorial cross as the right way to honor the overwhelmingly Christian identification of those who have died defending our country.

The intolerant reaction to crosses on various hillsides and mountaintops has nothing to do with a fear that non-Christians (like me) might feel unconstitutionally compelled to worship the emblem of the nation's majority religion. In truth, we remain blessedly free to view that symbol with indifference, respect, curiosity, devotion, bemusement or even contempt—in the same way that our Christian neighbors can look on displays of Hanukkah menorahs that have begun turning up on public property every December.

The campaign against religious symbols represents a war on memory itself.

A display of the cross (especially a cross that has been there for decades, such as the one in the desert) doesn't amount to "establishment of religion" or the imposition of theocracy, but it does function as a reminder of the fervent Christianity that has played such a potent, even predominant, role in shaping and sustaining this country. My Jewish kids aren't intimidated or threatened by such reminders, but they would be damaged by enforced ignorance of the Christian ideals and idealists behind crucial historical movements—from the pilgrims to the civil rights marchers, from the establishment of our most prestigious universities (nearly all of which began as Christian seminaries) to the battles to free slaves and resist international communism.

Reflecting a Christian Past

Of course non-Christians—including atheists, agnostics and members of minority faiths—have also played heroic roles in every era of the American past. But with the current freewheeling diversity in our religious marketplace of ideas—where missionaries for Scientology jostle the enthusiastic advocates of the Kabbalah Center—we're in little danger of viewing our culture's present or future in monochromatic or intolerant terms.

We do face formidable efforts, however, to erase and distort the nation's Christian past. In this sense, it's almost appropriate that secular activists focus on the crosses used in various war memorials: the very designation "memorial" derives from the word "memory," and the effort to obliterate these monuments in various locations amounts to more than a program to redecorate the landscape. The campaign against religious symbols represents a war on memory itself—and an intolerant effort to eradicate all prominent reminders of the faith-based heritage of this civilization.

6

No Clear Test Exists for Religious Symbols and the Establishment Clause

Avern L. Cohn and Bryan J. Anderson

Avern L. Cohn is a senior district judge for the US District Court, Eastern District of Michigan. Bryan J. Anderson is a lawyer in Detroit, Michigan. Both write for the First Amendment Center, an organization that studies First Amendment issues, including freedom of speech, of the press, and of religion, and the rights to assemble and to petition the government.

Colonial Americans sought to separate religion from government in the establishment clause of the US Constitution. Since then, the courts have hotly contested how to interpret the clause. The US Supreme Court has developed several legal tests. To withstand the Lemon *test, religious symbols on public land must have a secular purpose, must not advance or inhibit religion, and must not foster government entanglement with religion. The so-called endorsement test requires that government displays maintain neutrality toward religion. To meet the so-called coercion test, government displays must not coerce religious participation. Despite these tests, the courts continue to reach conflicting decisions. Because courts determine how to apply the establishment clause based on the facts of each case, predicting whether religious symbols on public land will violate the clause is a challenge.*

Avern L. Cohn and Bryan J. Anderson, "Ten Commandments, Other Displays & Mottos," First Amendment Center, June 2006. Reprinted by permission.

"Congress shall make no law respecting an establishment of religion . . ."

—*the First Amendment*

Those 10 words—the first phrase of the Bill of Rights—have been the focus of hotly contested debates and countless lawsuits—seeking to reach a consensus on precisely what the framers of the U.S. Constitution intended when they drafted what has come to be known as the establishment clause of the First Amendment. Interplay between religion and government is a decidedly sensitive topic, and determining just how much (if at all) one sphere can interact with the other is difficult and inevitably imprecise. . . .

The Legal Tests Used for Religious Displays

Thomas Jefferson is often quoted for his view that the establishment clause should be considered "a wall of separation between Church and State." Some justices on the Supreme Court seemed uneasy with that principle in some early cases when one described the United States as a "Christian country" in *Vidal [v. Girard's Executors]*, and another as a "Christian nation" in the 1892 decision *Church of Holy Trinity v. United States*. The Supreme Court of South Dakota as late as 1929 declared this a "Christian nation" and Christianity the "national religion" in the case *State ex rel. Finger v. Weedman*. Despite its early statements, however, the U.S. Supreme Court in *Everson [v. Board of Education]* reaffirmed Jefferson's view when it said, "The First Amendment has erected a wall between church and state. That wall must be kept high and impregnable. We could not approve the slightest breach."

The Supreme Court, nonetheless, later distanced itself from its statement in *Everson* that there is a "wall" between church and state when it conceded in its 1984 decision *Lynch v. Donnelly* that "the Constitution doesn't require complete separation of church and state." Public displays of religion have undeniably become embroidered into the tapestry of our lives so that it is practically impossible to go through a day without encountering some religious reference or symbol. Any transaction involving U.S. currency is a noteworthy example, as our national motto, "In God We Trust," has been imprinted on all U.S. coins since 1938 and bills since 1957. So how is a unit of government to know if a display involving religion is in discord with the establishment clause? An examination of the three tests the Supreme Court uses to examine religious mottos and displays (the *Lemon* test, the endorsement test, and the coercion test) is instructive but certainly not dispositive.

Lemon test. The Supreme Court in its 1971 decision *Lemon v. Kurtzman* synthesized its establishment-clause analysis when it pronounced a three-pronged inquiry commonly known as the *Lemon* test. To withstand *Lemon* scrutiny, the government conduct (1) must have a secular purpose, (2) must have a principal or primary effect that does not advance or inhibit religion, and (3) cannot foster an excessive government entanglement with religion.

Endorsement test. In addition to the *Lemon* test, the Supreme Court has also employed what is known as the endorsement test, a test that emphasizes government neutrality toward religion. In her concurring opinion in *Lynch*, Justice Sandra Day O'Connor, who is widely regarded as the Court's current leader in establishment-clause jurisprudence, introduced this second approach to analyzing potential establishment-clause violations when she noted two ways in which government can encounter trouble with the establishment clause: through excessive entanglement with religious institutions and through government endorsement or disapproval of religion. "Endorsement sends a message to nonadherents that they are outsiders, not full members of the political community, and an accompanying message to adherents that they are insiders, favored members of the political community," Justice O'Connor wrote. "Disapproval sends the opposite message."

In the 1995 decision *Capitol Square Review and Advisory Board v. Pinette*, Justice O'Connor clarified how the endorsement test should be applied when she said it must be applied according to a "reasonable observer" standard: "In this respect, the applicable observer is similar to the 'reasonable person' in tort law, who 'is not to be identified with any ordinary individual, who might occasionally do unreasonable things' but is 'rather a personification of a community ideal of reasonable behavior, determined by the [collective] social judgment.'"

Coercion test. At the other end of the spectrum of establishment-clause analysis, the Supreme Court has said that government action violates the establishment clause only if it coerces religious participation or support. Justice Anthony Kennedy advanced this so-called coercion test in the 1992 decision *Lee v. Weisman*: "[A]t a minimum, the Constitution guarantees that government may not coerce anyone to support or participate in religion or its exercise, or otherwise act in a way which establishes a state religion or religious faith, or tends to do so."

Choosing an Approach

Recent Supreme Court decisions demonstrate that there is not a consensus among the justices for a preferred approach to evaluate the constitutionality of potential establishment-clause violations involving religious mottos and displays. Although the Supreme Court has decided cases without expressly saying it was relying on the *Lemon* test, it perhaps is the most frequently and consistently used approach despite the fact that some legal scholars and justices themselves have criticized the test. Of the current Supreme Court, Justice Antonin Scalia is perhaps the most outspoken critic of *Lemon*. In the 1993 decision *Lamb's Chapel v. Center Moriches Union Free School Dis-*

trict, Justice Scalia likened the test to a ghoul in a horror movie that "repeatedly sits up in its grave and shuffles abroad, after being repeatedly killed and buried." Justice Scalia continued, "When we wish to strike down a practice it forbids, we invoke it, when we wish to uphold a practice it forbids, we ignore it entirely." Justice Scalia's criticism is notable because courts across the country have applied *Lemon* and the other tests to similar facts involving perceived establishment-clause violations and have consistently reached conflicting results. Indeed, attempting to determine what result a court will reach when deciding a case in this area of law is not an easy task. . . .

Attempting to determine what result a court will reach when deciding a case . . . is not an easy task.

Public Displays of Religious Symbols

Portraits of Jesus Christ

The 6th U.S. Circuit Court of Appeals did not use history to justify a portrait of Jesus Christ that had been hanging in the hallway outside the principal's office in the Bloomingdale (Mich.) Secondary School for 30 years. In *Washegesic v. Bloomingdale Public Schools* (1994), a student at the school sued, alleging the display of Warner Sallman's portrait, "Head of Christ," violated the establishment clause. The U.S. District Court found the display to violate all three prongs of the *Lemon* test, and the 6th Circuit agreed, saying "[t]he school has not come up with a secular purpose. The portrait advances religion. Its display entangles the government with religion." The defendants argued that the portrait "has meaning to all religions and that it is not inherently a symbol of Christianity." The 6th Circuit disagreed, acknowledging that the outcome of the case would be different if the school had included other symbols of world religions on the wall, "[b]ut

Christ is central only to Christianity, and his portrait has a proselytizing, affirming effect that some non-believers find deeply offensive." . . .

Holiday Displays

Because the establishment clause requires government "neutrality" in all things religious, numerous lawsuits have challenged the common practice of public holiday displays like crèches and menorahs, arguing that such displays are essentially government imprimaturs on a particular religion. In the 1984 *Lynch* case, the Supreme Court addressed the question of whether a crèche included in Pawtucket, R.I.'s annual Christmas display was unconstitutional. The Supreme Court's fact-sensitive analysis, which included an application of the *Lemon* test and Justice O'Connor's articulation of the endorsement test, concluded with a determination that the crèche did not violate the establishment clause. The Supreme Court said that the crèche display must be viewed in light of its setting, which included nearby traditional Christmas displays like a Santa Claus house, reindeer and a sleigh, a Christmas tree, lights and carolers. The Supreme Court viewed the crèche in the context of the Christmas season and noted that "the display depicts the historical origins of this traditional event long recognized as a National Holiday."

The Supreme Court reached a different conclusion regarding a crèche in its 1989 decision *County of Allegheny v. American Civil Liberties Union, Greater Pittsburgh Chapter*. In fact, *Allegheny* is particularly illustrative of the divergent views individual justices have taken when analyzing a holiday display. The case involved two such displays located on public property in downtown Pittsburgh: a crèche that was placed on the staircase of the Allegheny County Courthouse, and a display outside the City-County Building consisting of an 18-foot menorah celebrating Hanukkah placed next to a 45-foot Christmas tree (only the menorah was challenged in the case). The crèche was donated by a Roman Catholic group and featured a sign reading "*Gloria in Excelsis Deo*" ("Glory to God in the highest"). A sign saluting liberty was part of the menorah and Christmas tree display.

The justices' differing reasoning have led to disparate decisions by lower courts, as is frequently the case with establishment-clause challenges.

The Analysis

The Court analyzed each display separately and determined 5 to 4 that the crèche violated the establishment clause but 6 to 3 that the menorah display was not unconstitutional. The Supreme Court said that "*Lynch* teaches that government may celebrate Christmas in some manner and form, but not in a way that endorses Christian doctrine." Unlike that case, the Supreme Court said there was nothing in the surrounding setting of the Allegheny County crèche to detract from its religious message because the crèche was the *only* display on the courthouse's staircase. That, along with the fact that the staircase was considered the "most beautiful part" of the courthouse, led the Supreme Court to find that "[n]o viewer could reasonably think that it occupies this location without the support and approval of the government." Justices Harry Blackmun, William Brennan, John Paul Stevens and O'Connor joined in that conclusion, finding the crèche to violate the *Lemon* test because it had a "principal or primary effect" of advancing religion (Justices Blackmun and O'Connor also applied the endorsement test to find the crèche unconstitutional). Justices Anthony Kennedy, Byron White, Antonin Scalia and Chief Justice William Rehnquist found the majority's application of *Lemon* to reflect "an unjustified hostility toward religion" and would have allowed the crèche display based partly on the history of government participation in holiday seasons like declaring public holidays, erecting displays and hosting parades.

Regarding the menorah display, even though the menorah was the only item being challenged, the Supreme Court said it was necessary to consider it in relation to its surroundings, namely the Christmas tree and the sign. The Supreme Court noted that a Christmas tree is not itself a religious symbol, and that the 45-foot tree was the predominant element in the display. Accordingly, Justice William Blackmun wrote for the majority that the combination of the menorah and the tree indicated "not a simultaneous endorsement of both the Christian and Jewish faiths, but instead, a secular celebration of Christmas coupled with an acknowledgment of Chanukah as a contemporaneous alternative tradition." Moreover, the Supreme Court majority believed the sign further illustrated that the menorah does not serve to endorse Judaism but rather serves to recognize cultural diversity. Justices Blackmun, O'Connor, Kennedy, Rehnquist, White and Scalia agreed with this view, while Justices Stevens, Brennan and [Thurgood] Marshall believed the menorah display was unconstitutional because, in Justice Stevens' view, "the Establishment clause should be construed to create a strong presumption against the display of religious symbols on public property."

These cases and the justices' differing reasoning have led to disparate decisions by lower courts, as is frequently the case with establishment-clause challenges. . . .

Ten Commandments

Perhaps one of the most debated religious displays in recent years involves the Ten Commandments. Lower courts repeatedly have reached inconsistent conclusions with respect to the permissible public display of the commandments.

In the seminal Supreme Court case involving a public display of the Ten Commandments, the Supreme Court in 1980 struck down a Kentucky statute requiring that the Ten Commandments be posted on the wall of each public school classroom in that state. In *Stone v. Graham*, the state of Kentucky took the position that the statute had a secular purpose in that each display of the Ten Commandments contained small print noting that the display was posted to illustrate "its adoption as the fundamental legal code of Western Civilization and the Common Law of the United States." The Supreme Court, however, said the statute was "plainly religious in nature." The Court noted the Ten Commandments were not confined to a secular purpose, especially in light of their command to worship the Lord God alone.

In 2005, the Supreme Court revisited the Ten Commandments issue when it decided two significant cases involving these displays. Some legal scholars believed that the Supreme Court's grant of certiorari in these cases—*McCreary County, Kentucky, et al. v. American Civil Liberties Union of Kentucky, et al.* and *Van Orden v. Perry, et al.*—was an indication that the Court would attempt to clarify this increasingly murky realm of establishment-clause jurisprudence. When the Supreme Court issued the two respective opinions on June 27, 2005, however, the disparate results only emphasized the unpredictable nature of establishment-clause litigation.

Kentucky Case

In *McCreary County*, executives of two Kentucky counties—McCreary and Pulaski—posted large, gold-framed copies of the King James version of the Ten Commandments on the walls of their respective courthouses. The McCreary County display was placed in accordance with the county legislative body's mandate that the display be posted in a high-traffic area of the courthouse. The unveiling of the Pulaski County display included a ceremony led by the county's judge-executive, who called the commandments "good rules to live by" and invited the pastor of his church to speak at the ceremony. The American Civil Liberties Union of Kentucky promptly filed suit and sought a preliminary injunction against maintaining the displays.

Before the district court ruled on that request, however, each county installed a second Ten Commandments display, each of which stated that the commandments represented the legal code upon which the civil and criminal codes of Kentucky were founded. Each county's second display included eight other documents in smaller frames, each with a religious theme. The district court ultimately issued a preliminary injunction ordering that the displays be removed. Both counties, however, installed a third display in each courthouse, each of which consisted of nine framed documents of equal size (including the Ten Commandments, the Magna Carta, the Declaration of Independence, the Bill of Rights and a picture of Lady Justice). The third displays were titled "The Foundations of American Law and Government Display." The district court later supplemented the preliminary injunction to order the removal of the third display. The 6th U.S. Circuit Court of Appeals affirmed.

The Decision

In a 5-4 U.S. Supreme Court decision, Justice [David] Souter, writing for the majority, invoked the *Lemon* test and concluded that, in posting the first display, the counties had an unmistakable purpose of emphasizing and celebrating the commandments' religious message. He noted that a "reasonable observer," viewing the pastor's presence at the Pulaski County ceremony, could only reach such a conclusion. Souter also noted that the counties' subsequent displays—which contained additional religious and historic documents—likewise were constitutionally infirm. His majority opinion noted that the second displays' "unstinting focus was on religious passages, showing that the Counties were posting the Commandments precisely because of their sectarian content" and that the third display "quoted more of the purely religious language of the Commandments than the first two displays had done. . . . No reasonable observer could swallow the claim that the Counties had cast off the objective so unmistakable in the earlier displays." In holding the displays unconstitutional, the Court's majority opinion placed great emphasis on *Lemon*'s "purpose prong":

> "We hold only that purpose needs to be taken seriously under the Establishment Clause and needs to be understood in light of context; an implausible claim that governmental purpose has changed should not carry the day in a court of law any more than in a head with common sense."

Justice Scalia, writing for the dissent in *McCreary County*, criticized, as he has many times in the past, the application and continued viability of *Lemon*. "As bad as the *Lemon* test is, it is worse for the fact that, since its inception, its seemingly simple mandates have been manipulated to fit whatever result the Court aimed to achieve. Today's opinion is no different." Scalia said in dissent that the majority was wrong to characterize our government tradition as being one of religious neutrality and he drew a distinction between acknowledging a creator versus using public funds to aid religion or restricting the free exercise of religion:

> "[T]oday's opinion suggests that the posting of the Ten Commandments violates the principle that the government cannot favor one religion over another. That is indeed a valid principle where public aid or assistance to religion is concerned, or where the free exercise of religion is at issue, but it necessarily applies in a more limited sense to public acknowledgment of the Creator."

The Texas Case

In the second Ten Commandments case, decided on the same day as *McCreary County*, the Court in *Van Orden* held that the challenged display was constitutional. In *Van Orden*, the display consisted of a monument donated to the state of Texas by the Fraternal Order of Eagles in 1961. The monolith was located on the Texas State Capitol grounds as part of a display containing 17 monuments and 21 historical markers commemorating the "people, ideals, and events that compose Texan identity." The primary content of the monument was the text of the Ten Commandments. An eagle grasping the American flag, an eye inside a pyramid, two Stars of David, and the Greek letters Chi and Rho (which represent Christ) also were included on the monument. . . .

Former Chief Justice Rehnquist's plurality opinion first dispensed with the *Lemon* test, finding it "not useful in dealing with the sort of passive monument that Texas has erected on its Capitol grounds." Rather, the plurality's analysis focused on "the nature of the monument and . . . our Nation's history." Rehnquist cited what he labeled an "unbroken history of official acknowledgment by all three branches of government of the role of religion in American life from at least 1789," including both houses of Congress passing resolutions in 1789 to ask President George Washington to issue a Thanksgiving Day proclamation to "recommend to the people of the United States a day of public thanksgiving and prayer, to be observed by acknowledging, with grateful hearts, the many and signal favors of Almighty God"; as well as prior Supreme Court cases that acknowledged the history of religion in the founding of our country and the Supreme Court's courtroom itself, which the late chief justice noted has, since 1935, displayed a frieze showing Moses holding two tablets revealing portions of the Ten Commandments, along with images of other lawgivers.

Turning to the context of the challenged display, the plurality said the placement of the monument on the Texas State Capitol grounds "is a far more passive use of those texts than was the case in Stone, where the text confronted elementary school students every day." Justice [Stephen] Breyer, concurring in the judgment, wrote that *Van Orden* differed from *McCreary County* in that the McCreary County displays demonstrated "the substantially religious objectives of those who mounted them." . . .

The Dissent

Justices Stevens, [Ruth Bader] Ginsburg, O'Connor and Souter dissented. Souter, who wrote the majority opinion in *McCreary County*, was not persuaded that the expansive nature of the entire Texas display was indicative of constitutionality:

> "17 monuments with no common appearance, history, or esthetic role scattered over 22 acres is not a museum, and anyone strolling around the lawn would surely take each memorial on its own terms without any dawning sense that some purpose held the miscellany together more coherently than fortuity and the edge of the grass."

Although Souter recognized that the Texas display in *Van Orden* was unlike that in *McCreary County*, he nonetheless indicated that nothing could overcome the reality that the Ten Commandments constitute a religious statement. . . .

The different results reached in *McCreary County*—where the Ten Commandments displays were held unconstitutional—and in *Van Orden*—where the display was constitutionally permissible—likely will provide little predictability with respect to the disposition of future cases involving the Ten Commandments or other public displays of religious symbols. . . .

Courts, legal scholars and historians have grappled with the true meaning of the establishment clause ever since the Bill of Rights was ratified.

No Rigid Test

Courts, legal scholars and historians have grappled with the true meaning of the establishment clause ever since the Bill of Rights was ratified. . . .

Each federal court decision involving an establishment-clause challenge reflects a fact-sensitive examination and application of one of the modern tests used to resolve perceived government involvement with religion. Because of the number, structure, ambiguity and varied interpretations of the modern tests among courts and among Supreme Court Justices, attempting to predict the outcome of a particular case is an uncertain exercise. Although the Supreme Court has articulated tests to use when analyzing an establishment-clause challenge, they have not been rigidly applied. Certainly a rigid application would detract from the critical thinking and historical perspective required in constitutional analysis.

7

The Establishment Clause Does Not Ban Religious Symbols on Public Land

Ted Cruz and Kelly Shackelford

Ted Cruz and Kelly Shackelford represent the Veterans of Foreign Wars, the American Legion, the Military Order of the Purple Heart, and the American Ex-Prisoners of War. They wrote amici curiae, *friend of the court, briefs in* Salazar v. Buono, *a case before the US Supreme Court on the constitutionality of a war memorial cross on public land in the Mojave Desert.*

To achieve their goal of removing all religious symbols from public land, activists misinterpret the US Constitution. The First Amendment prohibits the government from favoring one religion over another by prohibiting the establishment of a national religion. The Constitution, however, does not say the government must be hostile to religion or faith. Indeed, former US Supreme Court Chief Justice Warren Burger held that opening a legislative session with a prayer is not the establishment of a religion but a recognition of beliefs widely held among Americans. Clearly war memorial crosses are not meant to establish a national religion. They allow Americans to reflect on the sacrifice of those who died to preserve their rights.

At Arlington National Cemetery near Washington, D.C., the Argonne Cross was erected to honor our fallen World War I soldiers. If you stand at the foot of that memorial, you cannot help but be moved by the sacrifices so many brave souls have made for our nation.

Ted Cruz and Kelly Shackelford, "War Memorials and the Constitution," *Wall Street Journal*, October 7, 2009. Reprinted by permission.

You will similarly feel deep admiration if you cast your eyes on row upon row of white crosses and Stars of David at the Meuse-Argonne American Cemetery and Memorial in France. Both fulfill the central purpose of our war memorials: They cause us to reflect on the sacrifices of American patriots.

Today, the U.S. Supreme Court will hear oral arguments in *Salazar v. Buono*, a case that will determine the fate of another moving monument to our fallen soldiers—a 75-year-old veterans' memorial located on public land in the vast Mojave National Preserve in San Bernardino County, Calif.

The Mojave Desert Veterans Memorial, a seven-foot metal cross, was erected in 1934 by World War I veterans to honor their fallen brethren. In 2001, the American Civil Liberties Union (ACLU) sued to have the memorial taken down. The reason? The ACLU claims that the mere presence of the cross within the 1.6 million acre national preserve runs afoul of the Constitution, because it is effectively a religious symbol.

Judge Robert J. Timlin of the U.S. District Court for the Central District of California agreed with that claim, and ordered that the cross be covered up while the case was on appeal. So now a memorial dedicated to those who fought tyranny and oppression is hidden from view by a plywood box.

That no religious symbol can be allowed on public land . . . is contrary to . . . how the Supreme Court has long interpreted the First Amendment's prohibition on the establishment of a religion.

A Disturbing Pattern

This case is part of a disturbing pattern. Like lawsuits seeking to stop the Pledge of Allegiance from being recited each morning in our public schools or to remove "In God We Trust" from our currency, the ACLU's argument in *Salazar v. Buono* is based on a misconception of the Constitution—that the government must be hostile to religion.

Far more is at stake than a single memorial. If the Supreme Court allows this cross to be destroyed, it could presage the destruction of thousands of similar memorials nationwide, inflicting sorrow on millions of Americans, especially veterans and their families.

The theory being advanced by the ACLU is that no religious symbol can be allowed on public land. That is a radical notion that is contrary to the text of the Constitution, to the original understanding of the Framers, and to how the Supreme Court has long interpreted the First Amendment's prohibition on the establishment of a religion.

The Constitution prohibits government from favoring one religion over another, but it does not compel hostility to faith. For example, the Supreme Court ruled in *Marsh v. Chambers* (1983) that it was constitutional to open a legislative session with a prayer. Chief Justice Warren Burger, writing for the majority, explained:

"To invoke Divine guidance on a public body entrusted with making the laws is not, in these circumstances, an 'establishment' of religion or a step toward establishment; it is simply a tolerable acknowledgment of beliefs widely held among the people of this country."

The Constitution prohibits government from favoring one religion over another, but it does not compel hostility to faith.

Likewise, in *Lynch v. Donnelly* (1984) the Court observed that "[o]ur history is replete with official references to the value and invocation of Divine guidance."

The Mojave Desert Veterans Memorial, like other war memorials, reflects the respect and gratitude due our honored dead. The men and women who have died defending our country gave their last measure of devotion to preserve our right to free speech and religious expression. They deserve our honor and admiration—not a plywood box marring their memory.

War memorials embody the very best traditions of our nation. In 1787, the U.S. Constitution was written to "secure the Blessings of Liberty to ourselves and our Posterity." With the case it will hear today, the Supreme Court has an opportunity to preserve this promise.[1]

1. On April 28, 2010, in *Salazar v. Buono*, a 5-4 decision, the Supreme Court overturned the lower court ruling that ordered the removal of the World War I memorial cross located in the Mojave National Preserve.

8

The Establishment Clause Should Not Be Used to Alter Historic Memorials

Michael Sean Winters

Michael Sean Winters is a political speechwriter and conservative political columnist for Catholic World. *He also writes a daily political blog for* America, *a Catholic magazine, and has appeared on television as a commentator. His political commentary has appeared in* The New Republic, New York Times, Washington Post, *and Slate.com, among others.*

To avoid claims that war memorial crosses violate the US Constitution's prohibition against establishment of religion, the US Supreme Court need not claim such crosses have no religious significance. The Court could have argued instead that there is no need to rewrite history. For example, when in the 1930s a cross was erected in the Mojave Desert as a memorial to World War I soldiers, America was referred to as a Christian nation. To claim that the war memorial cross has no religious significance simply makes it more difficult for those trying to interpret the meaning of the Establishment Clause and under what circumstances religious symbols on public land violate the Constitution.

One thing I confess I enjoy about some conservative commentators is that they never, ever sing out of tune. You turn to their analysis and you know what awaits you, the tired arguments, the links to Fox News, the misunderstood history,

Michael Sean Winters, "Salazar v. Buono: When Is a Cross Not a Cross?" *America*, May 4, 2010. Reprinted by permission.

the sweeping indictments. Mind you, there are plenty of conservatives who intrigue, who are not afraid to sing harmony, sometimes even a descnt, or even to question the suppositions of what is generally being pedaled. David Frum, Michael Gerson, Rick Garnett, Peggy Noonan and Peter Berkowitz are all conservative thinkers who surprise, engage, and educate with their arguments and their erudition. Unfortunately, most conservative commentary on the recent Supreme Court decision in *Salazar v. Buono* has been not just predictable, but juvenile.

In *Salazar v. Buono*, the Court was asked to decide whether a cross in the Mojave Desert, erected 75 years ago as a memorial to those killed in World War I, violated the Establishment Clause. There were six separate opinions in the case, but the governing decision was that of Justice Anthony Kennedy who wrote that the cross is "not merely a reaffirmation of Christian beliefs." He continued: "Here, one Latin cross in the desert evokes far more than religion. It evokes thousands of small crosses in the foreign fields marking the graves of Americans who fell in battles, battles whose tragedies are compounded if the fallen are forgotten." In dissent, Justice John Paul Stevens wrote that the cross "is a symbol of one particular sacrifice, and that sacrifice carries deeply significant meaning for those who adhere to the Christian faith."

No Victory for the Christian Faith

So, which of the two jurists better exemplifies secularization? The one who insists that the cross not be displayed on public land because it truly is of religious significance, or the one who permits the display of the cross because it has been gutted of its religious significance? Even if we like the outcome, we must deplore Kennedy's reasoning which tracks with the Court's rulings on nativity displays on public lands at Christmas. The creche passes constitutional muster if it is yoked with Santa and a menorah, that is, if the distinctive claim that Christmas makes (that God came down from Heaven and was born of a woman) is not emphasized but the invitation to generic jolliness (Happy Holidays Santa!) is emphasized. Call me silly, but such reasoning does not seem to me to be much of a victory for the Christian faith.

Yet, over at *First Things*, their "Gateway Pundit," Jim Hoft, begins his analysis "The ACLU [American Civil Liberties Union] went down in defeat today. The Supreme Court ruled that the Mojave Cross can stay." Oh, well, if the ACLU is upset, it must be a good thing—huh? He then adds that the decision was a "huge defeat for American communists." Did I miss the amicus brief from the American Communist Party? Is there still an American Communist Party? And, yes, there is the obligatory link to Fox News. With commentary like this, the magazine will need to change its name to *Trivial Things*.

There is no reason to go back into history and re-write it nor disturb its memorials.

Not to be outdone, over at the American Principles Project [APP] blog, the inimitable Thomas Peters also applauds the decision, writing, "The court has once again narrowly split in favor of the constitutionally-sound side of the question posed to it. Four justices—including the one nominated by [President Barack] Obama—voted against this lone cross in the middle of the dessert." Maybe if the "lone cross" had been in the middle of the appetizer or the soup, the Obama-nominated justice might have voted for it. Typos aside, which American principle in Kennedy's decision does the APP wish to applaud? Maybe they see this as a step towards an improved jurisprudence, but then they should make that case, not simply provide a knee-jerk defence of anything an Obama-nominated justice votes against. As I say, juvenile.

What the Court Might Have Said

Here is a stab at what the conservatives might have said in this case. The Court might simply have noted that in the

1930's, when the memorial to World War I soldiers was built, it was common to call America a "Christian country" and so such symbolism was to be expected, that this is part of our history and the first step of any assault on human dignity and freedom is the re-writing of history, that we would not allow a new display that was so specifically sectarian but there is no reason to go back into history and re-write it nor disturb its memorials. We need not say that Paul Revere saw two lanterns in the steeple of a tall building in Boston: He saw them in the steeple of the Old North Church. We need not drop the "Reverend" from our descriptions of patriot John Witherspoon. We need not efface the Celtic Cross at Gettysburg, which commemorates the "Fighting Irish" brigade.

I suspect many liberals could support such an argument too. Every battle need not be Armageddon, and not every cause espoused or opposed by the ACLU is a good cause, and, yes, the Supreme Court's jurisprudence on the Establishment Clause is in an ideological cul-de-sac from which it does not know how to emerge. There is much to discuss in all this, but it would be nice to find some smart, thoughtful conservatives, especially religious conservatives, taking a whack at it instead of the insta-punditry offered by the shills.

9

War Memorial Crosses Dishonor Veterans of Other Faiths

Sandhya Bathija

Before Sandhya Bathija became a communications associate for Americans United for Separation of Church and State, she worked as a reporter for The National Law Journal *and practiced law for a small civil rights firm in Detroit, Michigan. She writes regularly for* Church & State, *the magazine of Americans United, and for the organization's blog,* The Wall of Separation.

The use of crosses to honor the memory of America's fallen soldiers offends some veterans. Because many veterans are not Christian, to use a cross as a war memorial makes some veterans feel like outsiders. Although crosses on public land violate the constitutional separation of church and state, groups trying to prevent their removal assert that war memorial crosses are a symbol of patriotism, not Christianity. Many veterans staunchly oppose this view, arguing that using a cross as a veterans' memorial does not make the cross secular. Veterans support using crosses and other religious symbols to mark individual graves, but to use a cross to symbolize the sacrifice of fallen soldiers should recognize the beliefs of all, not just those who are Christian.

Fifty-five years ago, a 43-foot Latin cross was dedicated to "Our Lord and Savior Jesus Christ" during a religious ceremony on a hill in San Diego.

Sandhya Bathija, "Cross Purposes," *Church & State*, Americans United for Separation of Church and State, vol. 62, no. 2, February 2009, p. 7. Reprinted by permission.

Unveiled on Easter Sunday, the towering emblem serves as a site for Easter Sunrise services, prayer meetings, religious events and Christian weddings and baptisms, as many would expect.

An Unexpected Veterans' Memorial

The cross, which stands on public land, also serves as the government's chosen symbol to honor deceased military veterans for their service—something that Vietnam veteran Rich Gillock would never expect.

"The country that I took an oath to preserve, protect and defend did not demand religious conformity from everyone," said Gillock, an Orange County, Calif., resident. "This cross as a memorial doesn't really line up with what we believe in this country, which is that we are free to practice whatever religion we choose and the government should not have anything to do with it.

To many veterans, the Mt. Soledad cross is offensive, declaring that non-Christian veterans are outsiders and failing to honor them for the service they provided to their country.

"I don't even see it as truly a veterans' memorial," he continued. "There are a lot of veterans who are not Christian."

This Latin cross has been at the center of an ongoing debate for 20 years. Made of steel-reinforced concrete, it stands atop an 822-foot hill that is part of the Mt. Soledad Nature Park, a government facility that has been dedicated as a veterans' memorial since 1914.

To many veterans, the Mt. Soledad cross is offensive, declaring that non-Christian veterans are outsiders and failing to honor them for the service they provided to their country.

"A memorial should signify the return or safety of the men in service," said World War II veteran Bob Zweiman, former National Commander of the Jewish War Veterans of the United States of America. "But this does not represent the diversity of the military."

According to information provided by the U.S. Department of Defense, 29 percent of those currently serving in the U.S. military are not Christian. To many veterans, using Christianity's central symbol as a veterans' memorial is just another example of government favoring one religious belief over others.

"It sends the wrong message," said Vietnam veteran Dennis Mansker, president of Americans United's South Sound Chapter in Washington state. "There is nothing they could do at a war memorial that would take away from feelings for what I have done for this country, but this memorial does offend me, as if I am being put upon, and that one religious belief is trying to overwhelm others."

Evading Court Rulings

Despite this discomfort echoed by many veterans, and the fact that nearly one in three American soldiers is not Christian, the city of San Diego, the Mt. Soledad Memorial Association and a coalition of Religious Right organizations have pushed for this cross to stay standing, while evading years of court rulings that demand it be removed.

Religious Right groups have tried to depict the controversy over the Mt. Soledad cross as an attack on religion. Horace Cooper, senior fellow for the right-wing American Civil Rights Union, argued in an op-ed for *The Washington Times* that the Mt. Soledad cross should remain because it "reinforces religious freedom" and honors "our Christian heritage."

"Unfortunately, for some this heritage is merely a worrisome nuisance, particularly when it involves the cross," wrote Cooper. "Despite the sacrifice and bravery and overt religious motivations of so many of the earliest immigrants to our land, groups like the American Civil Liberties Union continue to pursue their efforts to suppress that memory."

Yet when it comes to defending the cross in court, the Mt. Soledad Memorial Association and its allies seem to suppress the memory that the cross is a Christian symbol. According to William Kellogg, president of the Mt. Soledad Memorial Association, the memorial has always been for veterans, not Christians.

The Mt. Soledad cross is unconstitutional and an inappropriate memorial for veterans in a religiously diverse nation.

Until recently, no court had ever bought that argument. But in July [2008], U.S. District Judge Larry Alan Burns said the Latin cross sends a non-religious message of "military service, death and sacrifice." Burns ruled the Latin cross could stay standing because it is not a religious symbol, but rather a symbol of American patriotism.

The American Civil Liberties Union [ACLU] filed an appeal on behalf of the Jewish War Veterans and other individuals to overturn the lower court's decision. In the late 1980s, the Jewish War Veterans successfully sued in *Jewish War Veterans v. United States* to have a Latin cross removed from federal property at Hawaii's Camp H.M. Smith and hopes this case brings about the same result.

"The cross ostensibly stands as a war memorial to all veterans, although it is a symbol of one specific religion and not of the diversity of religions to which our veterans' community belongs and has belonged since the earliest days of our country," the group says on its Web site. "All of the court decisions in such cases, including the final decision in the Camp Smith case, have upheld the principle that such a display represents a violation of the separation of church and state."

Americans United [AU] filed a friend-of-the-court brief on Jan. 14 [2009] arguing that the Mt. Soledad cross is unconstitutional and an inappropriate memorial for veterans in a religiously diverse nation. Joining Americans United on the brief are Hadassah, the Women's Zionist Organization of America; Interfaith Alliance; Military Association of Atheists and Freethinkers; Military Religious Freedom Foundation; Progressive Christians Uniting; and the Unitarian Universalist Association.

"That the cross is used in a veterans' memorial here does not make it secular," asserts the brief. "In fact, as a burial marker, the cross has been used almost exclusively for Christian burials in order to convey a sectarian message—that the deceased lived and died as a member of a particular Christian community. And as a monument in a veterans' memorial, the cross conveys a similar sectarian message: that only fallen Christian soldiers are being remembered. Given the 'commanding presence' of the Mt. Soledad cross in relation to the rest of the memorial, the primary message that this cross communicates is religious, not secular."

Secularizing the Cross

Secularizing the central symbol of Christianity is the newest tactic by anti-separationist groups to preserve government displays of the cross and America's "Christian heritage." Americans United is trying to counter that legal movement, and hopes to stop it, beginning in the 9th U.S. Circuit Court of Appeals when the court hears the Mt. Soledad case.

AU's brief, prepared by AU Madison Fellow Jef Klazen in consultation with AU Legal Director Ayesha N. Khan and Senior Litigation Counsel Alex J. Luchenitser, explains that history "leaves no doubt that the cross is a uniquely religious symbol, one synonymous with Christianity."

The brief also describes how Judge Burns' attempted secularization of the Latin cross offends Christians who celebrate the cross as a central emblem of their faith.

"Not only is it impermissible for the government to tell non-Christians that they are unwelcome in their community by giving pride of place to Christian imagery," the brief asserts, "but it is equally improper for the government to tell Christians that their sacred symbols are fit for public display because they have been officially transformed into secular objects."

The controversy over the Mt. Soledad cross has a long history. The City of San Diego authorized the Mt. Soledad Memorial Association to erect the cross on city land in 1952. In 1989, the ACLU brought the first lawsuit to remove the cross, resulting in both the U.S. district court and the 9th Circuit ordering removal of the symbol.

Judge Robert R. Beezer, writing for the 9th Circuit in *Ellis v. City of La Mesa*, said the memorial was "a sectarian war memorial that carries an inherently religious message and creates an appearance of honoring only those servicemen of that particular religion."

After this decision, the city tried to avoid removing the cross by selling the land under the cross to the Mt. Soledad Memorial Association through a ballot initiative. Judge Gordon Thompson ruled this to be unconstitutional. Writing for the court in *Murphy v. Bilbray*, he said that the city "clearly show[ed] a governmental preference for the Christian religion" by "taking the position of trying to 'save' such a preeminent Christian symbol." The 9th Circuit later agreed with Thompson in *Paulson v. City of San Diego*.

A New Tactic

After a series of other similar tactics to avoid the court-ordered removal of the cross, three San Diego area members of Congress introduced a bill that would immediately transfer the memorial to the U.S. Department of Defense. In 2006, President George W. Bush signed the bill into law, giving the federal government ownership of the memorial and allowing the City of San Diego to avoid complying with court orders.

Rep. Duncan Hunter was the chief architect of the bill, which passed the House by a 349-74 vote and the Senate unanimously. He claimed the day Bush signed the bill was "a great day for America's veterans and the San Diego community."

"The president's endorsement of this legislation," he said, "validates years of tireless work and sends a clear message that America appreciates and respects its military men and women."

Thomas Bock, president of the American Legion, also praised Bush for "walking in the 'footsteps of founders (of the country)' in recognizing the sanctity of this veterans' memorial.

"The religious symbols that mark the graves and honor the sacrifices of our fallen heroes—a cross, a Star of David, or other identification of faith in God—are sacred to Americans," he said. "As a grateful nation, we must ensure that the memory of our heroes will never be dishonored by those who would seek to remove them."

Like many trying to "save" the Mt. Soledad cross, Bock confused a government-endorsed Christian memorial with religious markers on fallen soldiers' gravestones. Americans United has supported religious markers on individual gravestones, since individual soldiers' families can choose the symbol of their own religion or not choose any symbol at all.

In the past, Americans United successfully sued the U.S. Department of Veterans' Affairs for denying relatives of fallen Wiccan soldiers the right to inscribe their own religious symbol on government-issued memorial markers.

The Jewish War Veterans, a plaintiff in this case, also supports the use of religious symbols on individual headstones in federal cemeteries.

"The individual symbol on each grave is not to be construed as an endorsement of one religion over the others," the group says on its Web site. "The range of religions represented on these headstones is a testament to the religious diversity of this country. It is a pictorial representation that, in our country, service people from all religions have fought and died to defend ingrained principles of liberty and democracy which must be the ground rock of our Nation."

That is what the plaintiffs would like any veterans' memorial to do—represent the diversity of this country—but the Mt. Soledad memorial simply does not, said AU's Luchenitser.

"The towering cross, visible for miles around, sends a message that the government favors and endorses Christianity," he said. "It fails to honor the sacrifices of the many non-Christian soldiers who have given their lives in the service of their country."

Even the conservative wing of the U.S. Supreme Court has pointed to the Latin cross as a prototypical example of an unconstitutional religious display.

A Budding Trend

The outcome of the Mt. Soledad case is particularly important because of an apparent budding trend of courts finding that the cross is secular and upholding government display.

In Utah, the Utah Highway Patrol Association decided to erect 12-foot crosses along highways to memorialize state highway patrol officers who died in the line of duty. A federal district judge ruled in November 2007 that this was a permissible practice, ruling that the cross is a secular symbol of death.

The case was appealed to the 10th U.S. Circuit Court of Appeals, and Americans United also filed a friend-of-the-court brief asking for the lower court decision to be overturned.

Supporters of the Mt. Soledad cross are hoping that their losing record in the courts will turn around because they are dealing with a different defendant. A lawsuit against the federal government instead of a California local government is an easier hurdle, they say, since the religious liberty provisions of the federal Constitution are less explicit than the church-state mandates of the California Constitution.

But that may just be wishful thinking. In the past, even the conservative wing of the U.S. Supreme Court has pointed to the Latin cross as a prototypical example of an unconstitutional religious display, AU states in its brief.

"Courts have repeatedly recognized that the cross is a sacred symbol with profound religious significance," asserts the ACLU's appellant brief. "Before this case, no federal court had ever upheld the government's permanent display of a Latin cross on public land as constitutional."

With that knowledge, Americans United and its allies are hopeful that the 9th Circuit can finally put this 20-year controversy to rest.

"This is a time when American soldiers of all faiths and of no faith—Christians, Jews, Muslims, Hindus, Wiccans, atheists, and agnostics—are giving up their lives in Iraq and Afghanistan for their country," said Luchenitser. "The government should recognize their sacrifices in a manner that honors fallen soldiers of all faiths and beliefs about religion, instead of commemorating only those of the Christian religion."

10

War Memorial Crosses Symbolize Courage and Patriotism, Not Religion

Patrick Brady

Maj. Gen. Patrick Brady, US Army retired, was awarded the Medal of Honor for heroism in Vietnam. He was later the Army chief of public affairs.

Despite claims by those who want to remove religious symbols from public spaces, the Constitution does not prohibit war memorial crosses on public land. The cross erected as a war memorial in the Mojave Desert, for example, is not a symbol of Christianity. It is a symbol of the courage and sacrifice of those who in World War I fought to preserve, among other freedoms, the freedom of religion. Thus, the cross does not violate the First Amendment's establishment clause that prohibits Congress from establishing a national religion.

In a recent and rare victory for veterans, our Constitution and common sense, the Supreme Court ruled that a World War I memorial cross standing 76 years in the wilds of the Mojave Desert did not violate the establishment clause ("Congress shall make no law regarding the establishment of religion . . .") of the First Amendment.

In the latest outrage, thieves have literally ripped the cross from the ground in the Mojave National Preserve.

For an ordinary person, it is mind-boggling to believe that the presence of a cross could establish a religion; yet 44 per-

Patrick Brady, "High Court Makes Right Call in Cross Case," *My San Antonio*, May 14, 2010. Reprinted by permission.

cent of the justices, and every court en route to the Supreme Court did—further proof of lingering Neanderthal genes in humans.

Abraham Lincoln warned: "Don't interfere with anything in the Constitution. That must be maintained, for it is the only safeguard of our liberties." Ignoring Lincoln's wisdom, today's court jesters have interfered with the First Amendment, perhaps the most significant 46 words in the history of civilization, to legalize pornography and flag burning while denouncing Christmas, God, the Boy Scouts and prayer. They will not allow the 10 Commandments to be posted in American courtrooms—even though it is posted in the Supreme Court.

How to explain such lunacy? There are two dominant schools of thought on interpreting the Constitution: those who believe the Founders meant what they wrote and those who believe that the Constitution is what they say it is—an amorphous document subject to progressive morality, personal bigotry, current trends, fashions and similar circumstances in foreign countries. Never play poker with the latter; they will change the rules in the middle of a pot.

That is the meaning of a cross—courage, service and sacrifice.

The head of the spear for these amorphous constitutionalists is the American Civil Liberties Union. Within the ACLU are coffined vampirelike beings who go berserk at the sight of a cross.

Hidden from the public square, in dark courtrooms, they convince like-minded judges that crosses on public land establish a religion.

Of course, the cross does not establish a religion. It is an icon used on national flags and countless symbols across the world. It covers the remains of American warriors in many foreign cemeteries. Those crosses symbolize their courageous service and sacrifice for those freedoms; and that is the meaning of a cross—courage, service and sacrifice.

Because of their courageous service and sacrifice, many of those warriors wore Distinguished Service Crosses and Distinguished Flying Crosses. Do these medals establish a religion?

Veterans saved the Mojave cross. They live and die to protect and defend the Constitution. We need to drive a stake through these vampires' hearts and stop them from sucking the blood out of our Constitution.

11

War Memorial Crosses Symbolize Christianity and Endorse Religion

Geoffrey R. Stone

Geoffrey R. Stone is the Edward H. Levi Distinguished Service Professor of Law at the University of Chicago, where he served as dean from 1987 to 1994. He is the author of books on rights and liberties in the United States, including Top Secret: When the Government Keeps Us in the Dark, War and Liberty: An American Dilemma, *and* Perilous Times: Free Speech in Wartime. *Stone also is chief editor of a fifteen-volume series,* Inalienable Rights.

The cross is not a neutral symbol that loses its religious significance when used to commemorate America's fallen heroes. In fact, most dictionaries define the cross as a symbol of Christianity. Thus, the Supreme Court cannot effectively argue that a war memorial cross on public land is not a religious symbol so that it will appear objective when the Court has actually based its decision in deference to the values of the dominant—Christian—society. The Court was wrong in Plessy v. Ferguson *when it argued that racial segregation did not reflect attitudes of racial superiority, and the Court is wrong to argue that a war memorial cross is not unconstitutional government endorsement of Christianity.*

What do you see? [see box on following page]

Do you have much doubt about it?

Geoffrey R. Stone, "A Cross by Any Other Name," *Huffington Post*, April 30, 2010. Reprinted by permission.

Reproduced with permission from the author.

It could be the letter "t."

But suppose it is eight feet tall and erected by the Veterans of Foreign Wars on federal land to honor American soldiers who died in World War I.

What is it?

I checked a dozen dictionaries, encyclopedias, and similar sources. Here is what I learned. It is "a symbol of Christianity." It is "the best-known religious symbol of Christianity." It is "the principal symbol of the Christian religion." It is "an emblem of Christianity." It is "the most familiar and widely recognized symbol of Christianity." It is "the symbol of Christian faith." It is "the cross of Christ's crucifixion."

There doesn't seem to be much doubt about it.

> *The inherent message of the cross is not a neutral testament to fallen heroes, but a potent affirmation by government of the Christian religion.*

Distorting the Meaning of Symbols

Except to some of the justices on the Supreme Court of the United States. According to Justice Anthony Kennedy, joined by Chief Justice John Roberts and Justice Samuel Alito, in this week's [April 2010] decision in *Salazar v. Buono*, the "cross is not merely a reaffirmation of Christian beliefs. It is a symbol often used to honor and respect those whose heroic acts, noble contributions, and patient striving help secure an honored place in history for this Nation and its people. [. . .] It evokes thousands of small crosses in foreign fields marking the graves of Americans who fell in battles, battles whose tragedies are compounded if the fallen are forgotten."

So, it's *not* "a symbol of Christianity"? It's *not* "the principal symbol of the Christian religion"? It's *not* "the symbol of Christian faith"? It's *not* "the cross of Christ's crucifixion"? It's a neutral symbol that just happens to be "used to honor [. . .] those whose heroic acts [. . .] help secure an honored place in history for this Nation."

And the American flag doesn't symbolize America? And the swastika doesn't symbolize Nazism? And a burning cross doesn't symbolize the KKK [Ku Klux Klan]? And the Golden Arches don't symbolize McDonald's?

In its 1896 decision in *Plessy v. Ferguson*, the Supreme Court upheld the constitutionality of racial segregation. In so doing, the Court considered the symbolic meaning of the legally mandated separation of blacks and whites into "colored only" and "white only" railroad cars: "We consider the underlying fallacy of the plaintiff's argument to consist in the assumption that the enforced separation of the two races stamps the colored race with a badge of inferiority. If this be so, it is not by reason of anything found in the act, but solely because the colored race chooses to put that construction upon it."

The Court is wrong in *Salazar* for the same reason it was wrong in *Plessy*: In both cases, the justices allowed meaning to be determined by the perceptions of the dominant forces in society, who like to imagine that their understanding of the world is neutral, natural, and objective. It is not.

The inherent message of segregation was not one of racial neutrality, but of racial subordination and inferiority. The inherent message of the cross is not a neutral testament to fallen heroes, but a potent affirmation by government of the Christian religion. This our Constitution does not allow.

12

Radical Secularist Attacks on Monument Crosses Threaten Religious Freedom

Newt Gingrich

Newt Gingrich, speaker of the House of Representatives until he resigned in 1998, is a scholar at the American Enterprise Institute, a conservative think tank. He writes regularly in support of conservative public policy and is the coauthor of Rediscovering God in America: Reflections of the Role of Faith in Our Nation's History and Future.

Radical secularists—those who want to purge religious symbols from all public places—actually threaten religious freedom. Efforts to remove a war memorial cross, for example, deny the religious freedom of those the memorial seeks to honor. The founders recognized that the right to religious expression comes from God, not from government. Thus, radical secularists and judicial activists should not be allowed to take away Americans' God-given right to unfettered religious expression and their right to erect crosses to honor their courageous war dead.

In the vast desert between Los Angeles and Las Vegas is the 1.6 million acre Mojave National Preserve. Located within the preserve, in an area so remote that an hour can pass between cars traveling by, sits a seven-foot cross on the top of a hill.

There used to be a cross there, that is. Today, the cross is covered by a plywood box, looking for all the world like a blank billboard on a lonely rock outcropping.

Newt Gingrich, "Radical Secularists Won't Allow a Cross in the Desert," *Washington Examiner*, November 27, 2008. Reprinted by permission.

A Target of Radical Secularists

The reason the cross is covered is as simple as it is dangerous: The cross is the latest target of radical secularists who seek to drive every manifestation of God and faith from our public spaces, however remote.

That these secularists would target a cross that sits literally in the middle of nowhere speaks to their fanaticism. That they would seek to destroy it speaks to their totalitarianism. For religious freedom to exist anywhere, it seems, is a threat to them everywhere.

For 75 years, what has become known as the Mojave Cross has stood on a remote outcropping in the desert known as Sunrise Rock. The cross was first erected in 1934 by the Death Valley chapter of the Veterans of Foreign Wars to honor the servicemen and -women who lost their lives in World War I.

Radical secularists . . . seek to drive every manifestation of God and faith from our public spaces.

For more than six decades, the cross stood, as it does at war memorials across the country, in memory of the American war dead. But about a decade ago, a park service employee in the preserve decided he was offended by the presence of a cross on federal land.

With the help of the American Civil Liberties Union [ACLU], he sued, arguing that the cross violates the constitutional prohibition on government establishment of religion. The 9th Circuit Court of Appeals—the same court that ruled the words "under God" unconstitutional in the Pledge of Allegiance—agreed and ordered the cross removed.

A Reasonable Solution

But then Congress got involved and came up with a solution. The land the Mojave Cross sits on was transferred from the federal government to the VFW [Veterans of Foreign Wars], thus removing the constitutional issue, for some, of a religious symbol on federal land.

But even that solution was not enough for the radical secularists. They've taken the case all the way to the Supreme Court, where justices heard arguments in the case earlier this fall.

It's anybody's guess how the high court will rule or if [it] will rule on the merits of the case at all. But it's clear to the nation's veterans what is at stake.

Literally thousands of other monuments and memorials on public lands display the cross and other religious imagery. If the court finds the Mojave Cross "offensive" for the ACLU and its allies, the crosses and other expressions of religious faith that honor our war dead elsewhere are in jeopardy as well.

It's a tragic irony that the men and women who died protecting our religious freedom may be denied theirs after death.

For the Founders, religious liberty and freedom of religious expression were indispensable supports to political freedom. But for the radical secularists, the truth is just the opposite: They see religious freedom as an obstacle to their political project to remake America into something our Founders wouldn't recognize. . . .

As we enter the Christmas season, it's important for Americans of all religious faiths to understand how important a cross in the desert—a cross they may never see—is to the survival of our liberty.

We are a nation founded on the truth that our rights come from God, not government.

If we give a handful of radicals and an imperial judiciary the power to decide that they, not our Creator, grant us our rights, we will be giving them the power to take our rights away.

13

Bad Reasoning of Activist Judges Allows Religious Symbols on Public Land

Bob Ritter

Bob Ritter is a staff attorney and legal coordinator for the Appignani Humanist Legal Center of the American Humanist Association, a progressive organization that believes people can lead ethical lives and promote the betterment of humanity without theism or other supernatural beliefs.

Some judges misapply the reasoning of US Supreme Court decisions in order to allow religious symbols on public land. Although a concurring Supreme Court opinion in Van Orden v. Perry *held that the US Constitution's establishment clause does not compel hostility to religion, the Court did not give governments the authority to allow private groups to put Christian symbols on public land. Higher courts should condemn a lower court case that misapplies the Supreme Court's reasoning in order to rule that Christian crosses placed on public highways to honor fallen officers have a secular, not religious purpose. The US Constitution expressly forbids such government support of religion.*

There is a new breed of judicial activism that ignores the prohibitions of the First Amendment and applies bogus reasoning to justify pro-religious rulings.

And it keeps getting worse.

Bob Ritter, "Bogus Reasoning at the Heart of Judicial Activism," *Humanist*, March/April 2008. Reprinted by permission.

For example, if I were to ask, "what do Xerox, Kleenex, and the Latin (Christian) cross have in common?" most people would probably struggle to find an answer. However, if you happen to be a federal judge, you may decide that each has become a common term—Xerox for photocopying, Kleenex for facial tissue, and the Christian cross for highway safety.

Haven't heard about the Christian cross-highway safety connection? You're not alone.

A federal district judge recently ruled in *American Atheists v. Duncan* that the state of Utah did not violate the establishment clause of the First Amendment when it permitted a private association to erect a number of twelve-foot-high Christian crosses with the Utah Highway Patrol beehive logo on them, on state-owned property to memorialize Highway Patrol officers who had died in the line of duty.

Most of the thirteen Christian crosses erected by the Utah Highway Patrol Association are located on government property—on highway rights-of-way, at rest stops, and a state office parking lot. These places are nonpublic forums and Utah law specifically prohibits persons from putting structures or objects within rights-of-way. Nevertheless the state of Utah, through its Division of Facilities and the Utah Department of Transportation, granted the private association permission to erect its memorial crosses.

There is a new breed of judicial activism that ignores the prohibitions of the First Amendment and applies bogus reasoning to justify pro-religious rulings.

Identifying Secular Purposes

In order to find that the Christian crosses did not violate the establishment clause, U.S. District Court Senior Judge David Sam had to find that the Christian crosses served a secular purpose.

Recognizing that "safety is a paramount concern to the people of Utah," Judge Sam evidently thought that the large Christian crosses rang a little safety bell in drivers' heads whenever motorists passed by. Had Judge Sam consulted the Utah Driver Handbook, he would have found that it doesn't show the Christian cross as one of Utah's traffic signs, signals, or road markings. It's safe to assume that the Christian cross is not a recognized symbol for highway safety.

There's more to Judge Sam's activism. He likens the so-called secularization of the Christian cross to the secularization of the Christmas tree. He's wrong on this one too. The Christmas tree has its roots [in] pre-Christian Teutonic religion. And the tree's religiosity is strictly dependent upon the addition of religious ornamentation. The "holiday" tree is, itself, secular. No religion owns the intellectual property rights to pine trees, red and green balls, or silver tinsel.

The bad news is that there is an upswing of poorly reasoned decisions favoring government participation in religion.

Judge Sam also said that the Christian cross "has attained a secular status as Americans have used it to honor the place where fallen soldiers and citizens lay buried" and that "Cemeteries throughout the United States, including cemeteries in Utah, display row upon row of crosses to mark the burial spot of those who served their community and their country." Not so. Brian Barnard, the attorney who is handling the case for the plaintiff, told me that it's neither true of cemeteries in Utah nor other cemeteries in the United States.

The fact of the matter is that the Christian cross is simply not a universal symbol. Judge Sam himself noted that 57 percent of Utah residents are members of the Church of Jesus Christ of Latter-day Saints and that they don't use the Christian cross "as a symbol of their religion or in their religious practices." Moreover, the U.S. Department of Veterans Affairs officially recognizes thirty-nine emblems of belief for placement on government headstones and markers.

Untangling Government and Religion

What this lawsuit is about, as so many are these days because of the frequent entanglement of governments into religious affairs, is ensuring that government—in this case the state of Utah—abides by the U.S. Constitution, which forbids government sponsorship of religion.

Our heritage is one of separation of government and religion. The Bill of Rights, ratified in 1791 prohibits governments from favoring one religion over another, or religion over nonreligion. Thomas Jefferson called this separation of church and state and the principle has served the United States well for over two hundred years.

Finally, Judge Sam misapplies the rulings of *Van Orden v. Perry* and *McCreary County v. ACLU* [American Civil Liberties Union], companion 2005 Supreme Court decisions. Quoting Justice Breyer's concurring opinion in *Van Orden* that "[T]he Establishment Clause does not compel a government to purge from the public's sphere all that in any way partakes of the religious." Judge Sam apparently sees *Van Orden* as a green light for governments to allow private groups to put Christian paraphernalia on public property under the bizarre reasoning that enforcing the establishment clause would constitute an impermissible hostility toward religion. Again, Judge Sam is wrong. It would appear that the *McCreary* decision—which involved a standalone Ten Commandments monument—would apply to Judge Sam's case.

While the bad news is that there is an upswing of poorly reasoned decisions favoring government participation in religion, the good news is that Judge Sam's decision isn't final, American Atheists plan to appeal the decision. And the Appignani Humanist Legal Center intends to file a friend of the court brief in support of the positions that the Christian cross is an exclusively religious symbol and the state of Utah endorsed religion and violated the First Amendment by permitting the crosses to be erected on public property.

14

The Courts Struggle over When to Allow Religious Symbols on Public Land

Ira C. Lupu, David Masci, and Robert W. Tuttle

Ira C. Lupu, professor of law at George Washington University Law School, is a nationally recognized scholar in constitutional law, with an emphasis on the religion clauses of the First Amendment. David Masci, one of the Pew Forum's senior editors, is a scholar at the Pew Forum on Religion & Public Life where he is an expert on culture war issues, including religious displays. Robert W. Tuttle is professor of law and religion at George Washington University Law School and, along with Ira C. Lupu, is co-director of the Project on Law and Religious Institutions.

Most Americans approve of religious holiday displays on government property. Whether the US Constitution supports these displays, however, remains unsettled. Clear divisions in the US Supreme Court have left the lower courts with no clear guidelines. Some justices believe the First Amendment's establishment clause forbids private citizens from placing religious displays on public property. Others are willing to allow religious displays in public spaces if such displays are open to everyone. Those who hold a middle ground assert that the establishment clause prohibits such displays only when they seem to convey that the government endorses the religious message. Clearly, the conflicting needs for government neutrality and religious expression are difficult for the courts; therefore cases are decided based on the facts of each case.

Ira C. Lupu, David Masci, and Robert W. Tuttle, "Religious Displays and the Courts," Pew Research Center's Forum on Religion and Public Life, June 2007.

Over the last three decades, government displays of religious symbols have sparked fierce battles, both in the courtroom and in the court of public opinion. Indeed, disputes over seasonal religious displays have themselves become an annual holiday tradition. Each year as the winter holidays approach, Americans across the country debate the appropriateness of the government sponsoring, or even permitting, the display of Christmas nativity scenes, Hanukkah menorahs and other religious holiday symbols on public property.

Polls show that a large majority of Americans support this type of government acknowledgment of religion. In a 2005 survey conducted by the Pew Research Center, 83 percent of Americans said displays of Christmas symbols should be allowed on government property. In another 2005 Pew Research Center poll, 74 percent of Americans said they believe it is proper to display the Ten Commandments in government buildings.

Early Court Cases

The Supreme Court first addressed the constitutionality of public religious displays in 1980 when it reviewed a Kentucky law requiring public schools to display the Ten Commandments in classrooms. The court determined that the Kentucky measure amounted to government sponsorship of religion and was therefore unconstitutional. According to the court, the law violated the First Amendment's Establishment Clause, which prohibits government from establishing a religion and from favoring one religion over another, or from favoring religion generally over nonreligious beliefs.

Four years later, the court took up its first case that specifically involved holiday displays. In that case, the court ruled that a Christmas nativity scene that the city of Pawtucket, R.I., had placed in a municipal square was constitutionally acceptable. The court stated that the nativity scene simply recognized the historical origins of the holiday, one that has secular as well as religious significance. In those circumstances, the justices concluded, the nativity scene did not reflect an effort by the government to promote Christianity.

Since these two decisions in the 1980s, the Supreme Court and lower federal courts have issued somewhat unpredictable rulings, approving some religious displays while ordering others to be removed. For instance, five years after approving the Pawtucket nativity scene, the Supreme Court ruled that a nativity scene on the staircase of a Pittsburgh, Pa., courthouse was unconstitutional. In that instance, the court concluded that, unlike the situation in Pawtucket where the crèche was shown together with more secular symbols, the Pittsburgh crèche was prominently displayed on its own and thus amounted to a government endorsement of religion.

The Supreme Court has . . . largely sidestepped setting clear rules that would assist lower courts in deciding future cases.

In 2005, the court ruled divergently in two cases involving permanent displays of the Ten Commandments. In one instance, the court decided that the relatively recent placement of the Ten Commandments in courthouses in two Kentucky counties violated the Establishment Clause because a "reasonable observer" would conclude that the counties intended to highlight the religious nature of the document. In the other case, however, the court ruled that a display of the Ten Commandments that had stood for more than 40 years on the grounds of the Texas state Capitol did not violate the Establishment Clause because a reasonable observer would not see the display as predominantly religious.

In reaching these decisions, the Supreme Court has relied heavily on a close examination of the particular history and context of each display and has largely sidestepped setting clear rules that would assist lower courts in deciding future cases. One result is a great deal of uncertainty about whether and how communities can commemorate religious holidays or acknowledge religious sentiments.

Deep Divisions

The lack of clear guidelines reflects deep divisions within the Supreme Court itself. Some justices are more committed to strict church-state separation and tend to rule that any government-sponsored religious display violates the Establishment Clause. These same justices also believe that, in some circumstances, the Establishment Clause may forbid private citizens from placing religious displays on public property.

Other members of the court read the Establishment Clause far more narrowly, arguing that it leaves ample room for religion in the public square. In recognition of the role that religion has played in U.S. history, these justices have been willing to allow government to sponsor a wide variety of religious displays. In addition, they have ruled that the Establishment Clause never bars private citizens from placing religious displays in publicly owned spaces that are generally open to everyone.

A third set of justices has held the middle and, so far, controlling ground. This group takes the view that a religious display placed in a public space violates the Establishment Clause only when it conveys the message that the government is endorsing a religious truth, such as the divinity of Jesus. For these justices, this same principle applies whether the display is sponsored by the government or by private citizens.

These divisions and occasional shifts have led to what many observers say are conflicting or inconsistent decisions on displays that are strikingly similar. Whether the appointments to the Supreme Court of Chief Justice John Roberts and Justice Samuel Alito will clarify the picture remains to be seen.[1] Regardless, the struggles over public religious displays have confirmed Justice Oliver Wendell Holmes' observation in 1890: "We live by symbols." He might have added that we fight over them too.

Divisions and occasional shifts [among Supreme Court justices] have led to what many observers say are conflicting or inconsistent decisions on displays that are strikingly similar.

Religious Holiday Displays

The Lynch *Decision*

A Christmas nativity scene in downtown Pawtucket, R.I., brought the issue of holiday displays to the Supreme Court for the first time. The case, *Lynch v. Donnelly* (1984), involved the city's sponsorship of an annual display of holiday decorations, which included a crèche (a manger scene portraying the birth of Jesus) as well as a Santa Claus, reindeer and other figures. The group of residents that brought suit argued that the Christmas display, and especially the créche, constituted government sponsorship of religion and thus violated the Establishment Clause.

In a 5-4 decision, the Supreme Court ruled that Pawtucket's display did not violate the Constitution. Writing for the majority, Chief Justice Warren Burger emphasized that government has long had the authority to acknowledge the role that religion has played in U.S. history. This authority suggests, he said, that the Establishment Clause does not require a total

1. Since *Van Orden v. Perry (2005)*, Supreme Court rulings have not in the eyes of most led to any significant clarification of establishment clause law. On April 28, 2010, in *Salazar v. Buono*, a 5-4 decision, the Supreme Court overturned the lower court ruling that ordered the removal of the World War I memorial cross located in the Mojave National Preserve. Chief Justice John Roberts concurred with the opinion written by Justice Anthony Kennedy, but Justice Samuel Alito, while concurring, wrote his own opinion. Justice Sonia Sotomayor, who joined the Court in August 2009, joined the dissent.

exclusion of religious images and messages from government-sponsored displays. He concluded that the local government had included the crèche to "depict the historical origins of this traditional event" rather than to express official support for any religious message.

Although Burger wrote for the court's majority, it was Justice Sandra Day O'Connor's concurring opinion that ultimately proved more influential, establishing the test that courts have relied upon in later cases. O'Connor declared that the Establishment Clause prohibited government from allowing religious belief or membership to impact a person's position in "the political community." Government endorsement of religion, she argued, elevates some persons to special status because their beliefs have been officially recognized and denigrates others who do not hold the sanctioned beliefs.

For O'Connor, government *endorsement* was the key factor. Courts, she argued, should ask whether a "reasonable person" would view the government's actions as an endorsement of particular religions. But while endorsement is prohibited, she argued, mere acknowledgement of religion, or of religion's role in the nation's history, is not.

O'Connor noted that in Pawtucket, the crèche was featured with a Santa Claus figurine and other secular holiday images. In such a context, she concluded, a reasonable person would not see the crèche as a government endorsement of Christianity but rather as one of a number of symbols that were relevant to a holiday that has secular as well as religious significance.

The strongest dissent came from Justice William J. Brennan, who argued that the city of Pawtucket had failed to demonstrate a "clearly secular purpose" for including the crèche. The other, nonreligious objects were more than sufficient, he reasoned, to reach the city's legitimate goals of encouraging goodwill and commerce. The crèche was added, he concluded, because city officials desired to "keep Christ in Christmas," and therefore the court could not say that "a wholly secular goal predominates" in the city's holiday display.

The Allegheny County *Decision*

Five years after *Lynch*, the Supreme Court returned to the question of seasonal religious displays sponsored by the government. The new case, *County of Allegheny v. ACLU* [ACLU is the abbreviation for American Civil Liberties Union] (1989), involved two different displays in downtown Pittsburgh, Pa. One featured a crèche that was donated by a Roman Catholic group and was placed on the main staircase of the county courthouse. The other was a broader display outside a city-county office building that included a menorah owned by a Jewish group, a Christmas tree and a sign proclaiming the city's "salute to liberty"; it did not include a crèche.

For the court, the case proved unusually divisive. In a notably splintered decision that included nine separate written opinions, the court found the display of the crèche inside the courthouse to be unconstitutional but approved the outdoor exhibit.

One group of justices (William Rehnquist, Antonin Scalia, Byron White and Anthony Kennedy) found both *Allegheny County* displays permissible. Echoing Burger's opinion in *Lynch*, the four justices argued that the Establishment Clause needs to be viewed through the lens of history, which has allowed for substantial government acknowledgment of religion. They argued that although government may not coerce someone to support religion, it should have significant latitude to passively acknowledge religious holidays. In *Allegheny County*, the four justices concluded, all of the displays, including the crèche, involved only that kind of passive recognition and therefore did not violate the Establishment Clause.

A second group of justices (John Paul Stevens, Brennan and Thurgood Marshall) concluded that both displays violated the Establishment Clause. They argued that the standard that should apply was O'Connor's test in *Lynch*—namely, whether a reasonable person would view the government's action as an endorsement of religion. In their view, both *Allegheny County* displays failed that test. Whether the displays include symbols representing one, some or all religions, the three justices reasoned, the Establishment Clause bars such endorsement. Religious symbols, they concluded, should be excluded from public displays unless the symbols are fully integrated into a clearly secular message. . . .

The court's decisions . . . are not easily reconciled.

Permanent Religious Displays

A second category of Supreme Court decisions focuses on permanent, rather than seasonal, religious displays that involve some form of government sponsorship. Most of these cases involve displays of the Ten Commandments.

The Stone *Decision*

The court's first such decision came in *Stone v. Graham* (1980), a case that focused on a Kentucky statute requiring public schools to post a copy of the Ten Commandments in every classroom. The state of Kentucky argued that the statute was designed to show students the secular importance of the Ten Commandments as "the fundamental legal code of Western civilization and the common law of the United States." But the court overturned the statute, concluding that the state lacked a plausible secular purpose for posting what the court saw as "undeniably a sacred text." An important factor in the court's decision was the public school setting. Courts have been especially wary of religious activity in the classroom because children are a captive audience and also are more impressionable than adults.

The Supreme Court returned to the issue of government display of the Ten Commandments in two cases decided on the same day in 2005. Rather than leading to clear, consistent rules, however, the sharply divided decisions in these cases further underscored the difficulty of the issues for local and state governments as well as for the courts.

The McCreary County *Decision*

The first case *McCreary County v. ACLU of Kentucky*, involved two Kentucky counties that had posted framed copies of the Ten Commandments in their courthouses. When a lawsuit was filed demanding that the Ten Commandments be removed, the counties expanded the displays to include several additional documents, each of which emphasized the important role of religion in American history and law. After a federal district court ordered the counties to remove the modified displays, the counties added even more documents along with a label: "The Foundations of American Law and Government Display." The displays included the lyrics to *The Star-Spangled Banner* as well as the texts of the Declaration of Independence, the Mayflower Compact, the Bill of Rights, the Magna Carta and the preamble to the Kentucky Constitution, plus documents explaining the displays.

Justice David Souter, writing for a 5-4 majority, stated that the two Kentucky counties had a religious purpose in posting the Ten Commandments in the courthouses, thus violating the Establishment Clause. Souter emphasized the principle of government neutrality among religions, and between religion generally and nonreligious beliefs. That principle, he wrote, ensures that religion does not ultimately cause political divisiveness and civic exclusion. The threats of divisiveness and exclusion are especially acute, he said, when government permanently and prominently displays a text that is unquestionably religious. . . .

Justice Scalia wrote the dissenting opinion in the case, asserting that the display of the Ten Commandments had a clearly secular purpose—namely, to demonstrate the role of religious teachings in the development of American law. The Establishment Clause, he stated, did not preclude government from recognizing the civic importance of religion. Moreover, he argued, the state should not be prohibited from acknowledging, and even favoring, the widespread belief in a single Creator.

The Van Orden *Decision*

The second case, *Van Orden v. Perry*, involved a challenge to the presence on the Texas state Capitol grounds of a stone monument inscribed with the Ten Commandments. The Fraternal Order of Eagles, a primarily secular group that erected similar monuments in other states and cities during the 1950s and 1960s, donated the display to Texas in 1961. It stood on the 22-acre Capitol grounds along with 16 other statues or memorials commemorating significant people and events in Texas history.

In *Van Orden*, a splintered court ruled that the Establishment Clause did not require Texas to remove the monument inscribed with the Ten Commandments from the grounds of its state Capitol. No single opinion received support from a majority of the court, but Chief Justice Rehnquist, in an opinion for a plurality of the justices, restated a common theme in cases involving the Establishment Clause. In deciding such cases, the chief justice wrote, courts must maintain a proper division between church and state, yet do so without "evinc[ing] a hostility to religion by disabling the government from in some ways recognizing our religious heritage."

In the chief justice's analysis, the display of the Ten Commandments on the grounds of the Texas Capitol was acceptable because the display constituted only a "passive" recognition of the country's religious heritage. The stone monument did not compel people seeing it to read the text, he said. Rehnquist also noted the monument's setting. Because the monument stood outside the Capitol, he wrote, there was little or no risk the state would use the text "to press religious observance upon [its] citizens."

Justice Stephen Breyer provided the fifth vote for the majority in *Van Orden*, but he did not join Rehnquist's opinion and chose to base his conclusion on narrower grounds. This is important because over the years, the court has consistently ruled that when no single opinion represents a majority of the court, the narrowest opinion that supports the court's decision is the controlling one. Because Breyer qualified his approval of the Texas monument with a set of limiting conditions, his opinion is narrower than that of the plurality and thus is the most significant guide for the lower courts.

In explaining his vote, Breyer did not focus on the government's authority to acknowledge religion's historical role in public life. Instead, he stressed the link between civic tranquility and government neutrality on religion. Breyer wrote that the Free Exercise Clause, which protects the right of religious belief and practice, as well as the Establishment Clause are intended to prevent religion from producing the kind of social conflict that would weaken both religion and government. To guard against such divisiveness, he argued, the government should neither favor nor disfavor any particular religion, or religion generally. But even some versions of neutrality can cause divisiveness, he wrote, as would happen if government sought to be "neutral" by completely banishing religion from public life. Neutrality must be tempered with tolerance for some religious practices that might run counter to an absolutist view of church-state separation. Such tempering, Breyer wrote, cannot be reduced to a simple, clear test; it requires the "exercise of legal judgment." . . .

In dissenting opinions, Justices Stevens, Souter, O'Connor and Ruth Bader Ginsburg argued that a reasonable observer would see the monument's text—with its large heading, "I am the Lord Thy God"—as an endorsement of religion by the state. They contended that the Texas monument was little different from the Kentucky courthouse displays that the court held unconstitutional in *McCreary County*. In both cases, they argued, the government failed to demonstrate a predominantly secular motive for the displays.

The court's decisions in these two cases are not easily reconciled. Together, however, the two cases suggest that it is the intent of those who put up a permanent religious display—rather than the display's effect—that determines if it is permissible. If the evidence points to a predominantly religious purpose, a display is likely to be found unconstitutional. If little or no such evidence is available—as may occur when displays have stood for decades—the courts are more likely to permit them....

Reconciling the need for government neutrality with the notion that public spaces should be open to at least some religious expression can be a difficult balancing act for the courts.

Looking Ahead

Given the important role religion plays in the lives of many Americans, it is all but certain that communities will continue to put up religious displays in public places. As a result, courts will continue to wrestle with the same two seemingly conflicting principles that have arisen in past displays cases. On the one hand, the Establishment Clause clearly prohibits the government from favoring any one religious creed or denomination, or from favoring religion over nonreligious beliefs. On the other hand, the Constitution permits the government to acknowledge the historical significance of religion in the nation's history and culture.

Reconciling the need for government neutrality with the notion that public spaces should be open to at least some religious expression can be a difficult balancing act for the courts. As the Supreme Court's decisions in the Ten Commandments cases illustrate, the ultimate outcome usually depends on the specific context of a display: its setting, language and history. Inevitably, however, contextual decisions lack the predictability that comes when courts apply rules that have clear, well-defined lines. But such rules might favor one core principle—government neutrality or acknowledgement of religion—at the expense of the other. Therefore, courts have largely focused—and likely will continue to focus—on the specific facts in each case, in the hope that their decisions honor both principles while still resolving the dispute at hand.

15

Promoting Religious Displays on Public Land Can Dampen Holidays

Sandhya Bathija

Before Sandhya Bathija became a communications associate for Americans United for Separation of Church and State, she worked as a reporter for The National Law Journal *and practiced law for a small civil rights firm in Detroit, Michigan. She writes regularly for* Church & State, *the magazine of Americans United, and for the organization's blog,* The Wall of Separation.

Although governments that allow a variety of religious symbols on government property during the holidays are upholding the constitutional separation of church and state, representatives of the Religious Right nevertheless stir up public unrest. They lead some to falsely believe that those who oppose these displays are leading a war on Christmas. Because of such overreactions, these pundits do more to dampen holiday spirits than those trying to urge governments not to promote one religious faith over others. Thus, the public protest that erupted when village leaders changed the name of a government-funded parade from a Christmas to a Holiday Parade put an end to the parade and any holiday spirit the village might have enjoyed from it.

Last holiday season [2008], Bill O'Reilly was fuming a little bit more than usual.

The bombastic Fox News host declared that Washington Gov. Christine Gregoire had "insulted Christians all over the

Sandhya Bathija, "How the Religious Right Stole Christmas," *Church & State*, Americans United for Separation of Church and State, vol. 62, no. 11, December 2009, p. 73. Reprinted by permission.

world" when she "allowed" a Winter Solstice display to stand next to a Christmas tree and a Nativity scene in the state's capitol building.

But what O'Reilly failed to acknowledge in his op-ed for *The Washington Times* was that Gregoire was just doing her job. She was enforcing a court order that stemmed from a case between the state and O'Reilly's friends at the Alliance Defense Fund [ADF].

The ADF, a Religious Right group, had represented a local man who wanted to erect a Nativity scene in the state capitol rotunda, forcing the state in 2007 to broaden its policy on displays.

That meant that when the next holiday season rolled around, the capitol rotunda had to be open to an atheist sign that stated, "At this season of the Winter Solstice, may reason prevail. There are no gods, no devils, no angels, no heaven or hell. There is only our natural world. Religion is but myth and superstition that hardens hearts and enslaves minds."

Every year during the holiday season, right-wing pundits and Religious Right groups rally their followers by claiming there is a 'war on Christmas.'

An Annual Rant

Even if he was aware of those facts, O'Reilly's rant came as little surprise.

Every year during the holiday season, right-wing pundits and Religious Right groups rally their followers by claiming there is a "war on Christmas." These groups are outraged annually by holiday displays, parades, music and anything else that has to do with the December holiday—unless a large dollop of Christianity is included.

Last year, it got so bad in Olympia [Washington] that protestors began gathering outside the Capitol demanding that the Solstice sign come down. The demonstrators attacked Gregoire, carrying signs that portrayed her as the Grinch.

The Rev. Ken Hutcherson, a Religious Right leader in the community, announced at the protest that the governor had "led the state of Washington to be the armpit of America. And I'm afraid that our governor is the one adding the offensive odor to the armpit."

After last year's debacle over religious symbols in the capitol rotunda, state officials have issued new permanent rules barring all nongovernment displays inside the Capitol campus building.

The Washington Department of General Administration signed off on the policy after listening to testimony at hearings in September [2009]. Dennis Mansker, Americans United's South Sound Chapter president, supported the proposed changes and provided suggestions for how the state should handle temporary displays on Capitol grounds.

The Hazards of an Open Public Forum

"We do not need a repeat of last year's holiday display embarrassment," he said. "Though we support free speech, we all learned the potential hazards of an open public forum. Our Capitol building should be used to carry out the people's business, which includes allowing people to petition their lawmakers. But space is limited, thus a prohibition on unattended displays makes perfect sense."

Despite the ban on displays inside the Capitol rotunda, the new policy still allows religious displays outside the Capitol campus buildings, which could move last year's dispute to the outdoors, Mansker said.

"As far as the new rule goes, I think it hasn't really solved anything," he said. "Now there will be Nativity scenes outside the Capitol building, which I think makes the problem worse.

Outdoor displays are by their nature more visible and therefore much more likely to give the impression that the state is supporting religion."

Situations like this are not isolated. As early as October this year [2009], a Michigan resident claimed religious persecution because the government would not permit him to erect a stand-alone Nativity scene on public land.

John Satawa claims he has placed the creche on the median of a public road in Warren, Mich., for decades. Last year, Warren's road commission rejected the Nativity scene because Satawa had not requested a permit. This year, when he asked ahead of time, he was officially turned down because the tableau "clearly displays a religious message" and would violate the First Amendment.

Satawa, represented by the Religious Right's Thomas More Law Center, filed a lawsuit challenging the city's decision.

A Michigan resident claimed religious persecution because the government would not permit him to erect a stand-alone Nativity scene on public land.

"Every Christmas holiday," said Richard Thompson, Center president and chief counsel, "militant atheists, acting like the Taliban, use the phrase 'separation of church and state,'—nowhere found in our Constitution—as a means of intimidating municipalities and schools into removing expressions celebrating Christmas, a national holiday.

"Their goal is to cleanse our public square of all Christian symbols," he continued. "However, the grand purpose of our Founding Fathers and the First Amendment was to protect religion, not eliminate it."

The Law on Religious Displays

Over the years, Americans United for Separation of Church and State [AU] has urged government officials to remember the Constitution when dealing with holiday displays. AU's legal department has sent letters to numerous city and county governments advising them on the law regarding creches on public land.

Expert advice about Nativity scenes is important because the law governing such displays is far from straightforward thanks to two U.S. Supreme Court decisions: *Lynch v. Donnelly* and *City of Allegheny v. ACLU.*

The 1984 Lynch case involved Pawtucket, R.I., which erected a Christmas display in a park. It included a Santa Claus house, reindeer pulling Santa's sleigh, candy-striped poles, a Christmas tree, carolers, some cut-out shapes of a clown, elephant and teddy bear, colored lights and a large banner that read "Seasons Greetings." The city also included a depiction of the birth of Jesus within this display.

City residents and the local ACLU [American Civil Liberties Union] filed a lawsuit to challenge the inclusion of the creche, which consisted of the infant Jesus, Mary and Joseph, angels, shepherds, wise men and animals. The high court, in a 5-4 decision, upheld the Nativity scene as constitutional. Because the display was accompanied by other secular holiday symbols, the court majority reasoned, it did not constitute a government endorsement of religion.

Chief Justice Warren Burger, writing for the court, said the city had "principally taken note of a significant historical religious event long celebrated in the Western World. The creche in the display depicts the historical origins of this traditional event long recognized as a National holiday."

The Burger court's decision was praised by the Rev. Jerry Falwell, who said, "This ruling portends good things for the future."

Falwell's then lieutenant, Cal Thomas, echoed that sentiment, claiming the high court had removed "religious Americans from second-class citizenship."

A Nativity Standing Alone

Civil liberties groups were disappointed but received some better news five years later in the *Allegheny* decision. For the first time the high court stated definitively that religious symbols standing alone at public buildings violate church-state separation.

The court considered two religious displays: a freestanding Nativity scene on the steps of a Pennsylvania courthouse and an 18-foot menorah outside the nearby city-county building, which was part of a display that included secular holiday symbols, such as a 45-foot Christmas tree.

The justices upheld the menorah. Writing for the court, Justice Harry A. Blackmun said, "The necessary result of placing a menorah next to a Christmas tree is to create an 'overall holiday setting' that represents both Christmas and Chanukah—two holidays, not one."

But the creche standing alone took things too far, Blackmun held.

"There is no doubt, of course, that the creche itself is capable of communicating a religious message," he wrote. "Unlike in *Lynch*, nothing in the context of the display detracts from the creche's religious message.

"*Lynch* teaches that government may celebrate Christmas in some manner and form, but not in a way that endorses Christian doctrine," he continued. "Here, Allegheny County has transgressed this line. It has chosen to celebrate Christmas in a way that has the effect of endorsing a patently Christian message: Glory to God for the birth of Jesus Christ."

These leading Supreme Court rulings have led to confusion about whether a Nativity scene can stand on public land.

Inevitable Disputes

That's why almost every year, disputes over creches are inevitable.

But it doesn't just stop with religious symbols. Religious Right groups find any means possible to stir up controversy over Christmas, trying to push "Christian nation" propaganda and arguing that civil liberties groups are censoring religious speech.

Catholic League President Bill Donohue issued a press release on Nov. 3 of this year headlined "War on Christmas Commences." In the release, he cited several instances, not just those regarding creche displays, showcasing how "cultural fascists" have tried to ruin Christmas 2009.

One of those instances involved a tree on the Capitol lawn in Frankfort, Ky. Gov. Steve Beshear initially dubbed a giant evergreen there as a "holiday tree," instead of a Christmas tree, angering some Christians in the state.

Almost every year, disputes over creches are inevitable.

The Rev. Jeff Fugate of Lexington said changing the tree's name offends Christians, and Republican Senate President David Williams said the governor was putting political correctness above Kentucky values.

In response to Religious Right criticism, the governor issued a statement inviting people to a "Christmas tree" lighting ceremony. A spokeswoman said Beshear always meant for it to be a "Christmas tree."

A similar dispute over a parade in Amelia, Ohio, has also angered Religious Right activists this holiday season. For 28 years, the Amelia Business Association had sponsored the parade, but this year, the organization wanted to hand over that responsibility to the village government.

Village Solicitor Laura Abrams said that since the parade was being put on with government funds, it could no longer be called a Christmas parade and changed the name to "A Holiday Parade."

Churches told the village they would boycott the parade because of the name change and some people threatened to hold demonstrations. A local township even said it would not participate in the parade and would close a portion of the parade route that ran through the township.

"Understandably," said Donohue, "this dishonest scheme created a furor, the result being—just to play it safe—there will be no parade."

In the past, this anger over "censoring Christmas" has led to massive fundraising campaigns for right-wing organizations. In years past, the Alliance Defense Fund sold "Christmas Packs" for $29 apiece, each consisting of a three-page legal memo and two lapel pins.

Liberty Counsel, an adjunct of the late Jerry Falwell's empire, and the Rev. Donald Wildmon's American Family Association provided a "Help Save Christmas Action Pack," selling buttons that say, "I ?? Christmas." The buttons are available again this year through the group's Web site.

Liberty Counsel, now headed by Liberty University Law School Dean Mat Staver, has also put together a "Naughty and Nice" list of retailers, based on the language stores use in their holiday marketing materials. The group recommends boycotts against stores that use "Happy Holidays" rather than "Merry Christmas."

New Tactics Every Year

After so many years, it comes as no surprise that every November, there is bound to be a new tactic put forth by the Religious Right to "save" Christmas. A California woman has come up with the latest.

Merry Susan Hyatt, a 61-year-old substitute teacher, has proposed a California ballot initiative that would require public schools to offer religious carols at Christmas. The measure states, "Each public elementary and secondary school shall provide opportunities to its pupils of listening to or performing Christmas music at an appropriate time of year."

Hyatt said she was shocked by a holiday celebration at a school where she was a substitute.

"We were having Christmas without Jesus," she told New America Foundation, describing her surprise that a school can prohibit the singing of religiously themed music at school performances, including winter recitals.

Hyatt said she isn't much concerned about people of other faiths who may take offense at the Christian music. As a substitute teacher, Hyatt said she primarily works in heavily Latino, largely Christian neighborhoods in Southern California.

"I don't think I've ever had a Jewish child in one of my classes," she told *The New York Times*. "If so, they never said anything."

Hyatt will need 434,000 valid signatures by March 29 to put the initiative on the November 2010 ballot—meaning, the Religious Right has a new project to play up.

In the meantime, these groups are sure to keep fighting for unconstitutional religious displays on public land, as well as complaining about the use of the word "holiday" instead of "Christmas," among other grievances.

Separating Church and State

In response, AU will continue to keep church and state separate during the holiday season, just as it does throughout the year.

"Christmas and the Constitution can easily co-exist," said the Rev. Barry W. Lynn, Americans United executive director. "We are simply urging government officials to follow the law, which bars government from promoting one religious faith over others.

"If officials decide to put up holiday decorations at Christmas," he continued, "they must do so in a way that does not give government support to Christianity. America is an incredibly diverse nation, and government should never send the message that one faith is the officially preferred one."

Organizations to Contact

The editors have compiled the following list of organizations concerned with the issues debated in this book. The descriptions are derived from materials provided by the organizations. All have publications or information available for interested readers. The list was compiled on the date of publication of the present volume; the information provided here may change. Be aware that many organizations take several weeks or longer to respond to inquiries, so allow as much time as possible.

American Civil Liberties Union (ACLU)
125 Broad St., 18th Floor, New York, NY 10004
(212) 549-2500
website: www.aclu.org

The ACLU is a large national organization that works to preserve First Amendment rights—freedom of speech, freedom of association and assembly, freedom of the press, and freedom of religion supported by the strict separation of church and state—as well as the right to equal protection under the law regardless of race, sex, religion, or national origin. Its website offers news and legal briefs concerning religious symbols on public land, including amicus briefs from the ACLU and other organizations submitted to the Supreme Court in *Salazar v. Buono.*

Americans for Religious Liberty (ARL)
PO Box 6656, Silver Spring, MD 20916
(301) 260-2988 • fax: (301) 260-2989
e-mail: arlinc@verizon.net
website: www.arlinc.org

The mission of ARL is to defend the core constitutional principle of separation of church and state. In its quarter century of activism in defense of church-state separation and freedom of conscience, it has been involved in more than 60 actions in the courts, a summary of which can be found on its website. ARL publishes the quarterly newsletter, *The Voice of Reason*, recent and back issues of which are available on its website. The ARL website also provides access to articles such as "That Wall" and print publications that can be purchased by mail, including *The Separation of Church and State: Writings on a Fundamental Freedom by America's Founders* and *The December Wars: Religious Symbols and Ceremonies in the Public Square.*

Americans United for Separation of Church and State (AU)
518 C St. NE, Washington, DC 20002
(202) 466-3234 • fax: (202) 466-2587
e-mail: americansunited@au.org
website: www.au.org

AU is an independent nonprofit organization that protects the separation of church and state by working on a wide range of pressing political and social issues. As a nonsectarian, nonpartisan organization, AU's membership includes Christians, Jews, Buddhists, people with no religious affiliation, and others. It publishes the monthly magazine *Church & State*, which includes articles about court cases and other news concerning, among other issues, religious symbols on public land. On its website, AU publishes articles from *Church & State*, comments on its *The Wall of Separation* blog, and printable brochures, including "Is America a Christian Nation?"

Brookings Institution
1775 Massachusetts Ave. NW, Washington, DC 20036
(202) 797-6000 • fax: (202) 797-6004
e-mail: brookinfo@brook.edu
website: www.brookings.edu

The Brookings Institution is devoted to nonpartisan research, education, and publication in economics, government, foreign policy, and the social sciences. Its principal purposes are to aid in the development of sound public policies and to promote public understanding of issues of national importance. It publishes the quarterly journal the *Brookings Review*, which periodically includes articles that explore issues related to the free exercise and establishment clauses of the First Amendment. On its website, the institution publishes articles about Supreme Court decisions regarding separation of church and state, including "God in Government: Judge Sotomayor's Church-State Record" and "Justice Souter and Supreme Court's Church-State Balance."

Cato Institute

1000 Massachusetts Ave. NW, Washington, DC 20001-5403
(202) 842-0200 • fax: (202) 842-3490
e-mail: cato@cato.org
website: www.cato.org

The Cato Institute is a libertarian public policy research foundation that aims to limit the role of government and protect civil liberties. The institute publishes the quarterlies, *CATO Journal* and *Regulation*, the bimonthly *Cato Policy Report*, and the annual *CATO Supreme Court Review*. Its website publishes selections from these and other publications, including "*Pleasant Grove City v. Summum*: The Supreme Court Finds Public Display of the Ten Commandments to Be Permissible Government Speech."

Family Research Council (FRC)

810 G St. NW, Washington, DC 20001
(202) 393-2100 • fax: (202) 393-2134
website: www.frc.org

FRC is an organization that advances the importance of faith, family, and freedom in public policy. It promotes these core values through policy research, public education, and grassroots mobilization. FRC publishes books and pamphlets on these issues, many of which are available on its website, including "Another Look at Jefferson's Wall of Separation: A Jurisdictional Interpretation of the 'Wall' Metaphor" and "Debating Church and State in Texas."

First Amendment Center

1207 18th Ave. S, Nashville, TN 37212
(615) 727-1600 • fax: (615) 727-1319
e-mail: info@fac.org
website: www.firstamendmentcenter.org

The First Amendment Center, which is affiliated with Vanderbilt University, works to preserve and protect First Amendment freedoms through information and education. The center serves as a forum for the study and exploration of free-expression issues, including freedom of speech, of the press, and of religion, and the rights to assemble and to petition the government. It publishes the five-volume book, *The Law of Church and State in America*, periodic *State of the First Amendment* surveys, reports, and articles, including "Ten Commandments, Other Displays & Mottos" and "Religious Liberty in Public Life," all of which are available on its website.

Freedom from Religion Foundation (FFRF)

PO Box 750, Madison, WI 53701
(608) 256-8900 • fax: (608) 204-0422
website: www.ffrf.org

FFRF is an advocacy group established on the premise that most social and moral progress has been brought about by persons free from religion. Committed to the principle of separation of state and church, FFRF advocates on issues such as prison reform, the humane treatment of the mentally ill, the abolition of capital punishment, death with dignity, and the right to choose contraception, sterilization, and abortion, among others. In addition to its *Nontracts*, the foundation's answer to religious tracts, FFRF publishes books, brochures, and the monthly *Freethought Today*, selected articles from which are published on its website, including "Wall of Separation Requires Vigilance." The foundation also publishes answers to Frequently Asked Questions such as "Are Christmas Displays a Violation of the First Amendment?"

The Heritage Foundation
214 Massachusetts Ave. NE, Washington, DC 20002-4999
(202) 546-4400 • fax: (202) 546-8328
e-mail: info@heritage.org
website: www.heritage.org

Founded in 1973, The Heritage Foundation is a conservative research and educational institute, whose mission is to formulate and promote conservative public policies based on the principles of free enterprise, limited government, and individual freedom. It publishes numerous books, reports, factsheets, commentary, and testimony on foreign and domestic policy and religious freedom, including "Holiday Naysayers," "The War on Christmas," and "God and Man at the Supreme Court: Rethinking Religion in Public Life."

North American Religious Liberty Association (NARLA)
101 W Cochran St., Simi Valley, CA 93065
(805) 955-7675
e-mail: narla@religiousliberty.info
website: www.religiousliberty.info

NARLA, which is affiliated with the Seventh-Day Adventist Church, exists to ensure that all peaceful people of faith are accorded the fundamental right not only to hold their beliefs but also to actively practice their faith. It also works to ensure that religion is not co-opted by the state through direct regulation or through financial control. It publishes the monthly magazine *Liberty*, which contains articles about religious freedom; archives are available at www.libertymagazine.org.

People for the American Way
2000 M St. NW, Suite 400, Washington, DC 20036
(202) 467-4999
e-mail: pfaw@pfaw.org
website: www.pfaw.org

People for the American Way is a nonprofit educational organization that is engaged in lobbying and other forms of political activism. Its purpose is to affirm "the American Way," by which it means pluralism; individuality; freedom of thought, expression, and religion; a sense of community; and tolerance and compassion for others. It is strongly opposed to the views of the Religious Right and favors a high wall of separation between church and state. Its website contains reports and press releases about recent and upcoming court cases that involve, among other issues, religious displays on public land, including "The Religious Right's Bizarre Understanding of the Establishment Clause" and "Supreme Court Weakens First Amendment."

Pew Forum on Religion and Public Life
1615 L St. NW, Suite 700, Washington, DC 20036
(202) 419-4550 • fax: (202) 419-4559
website: http://pewforum.org

The Pew Forum on Religion and Public Life in a nonpartisan, nonadvocacy organization that seeks to promote a deeper understanding of issues at the intersection of religion and public affairs. It pursues its mission by delivering timely, impartial information to national opinion leaders, including government officials and journalists, but does not take positions on policy debates. On its website the forum publishes surveys, event transcripts, reports, and articles, including "High Court Decision in *Salazar v. Buono*," "Analysis of Ten Commandments Decisions," and "From the Ten Commandments to Christmas Trees: Public Religious Displays and the Courts."

Bibliography

Books

David M. Ackerman, Kimberly D. Jones, and Christopher A. Jennings	*The Law of Church and State in the Supreme Court*. New York: Nova Science Publishers, 2003.
Casey Nelson Blake, ed.	*The Arts of Democracy: Art, Public Culture, and the State*. Washington, DC: Woodrow Wilson Center Press, 2007.
John C. Blakeman	*The Bible in the Park: Religious Expression, Public Forums, and Federal District Courts*. Akron, OH: University of Akron Press, 2005.
Rob Boston	*Why the Religious Right Is Wrong About Separation of Church & State*. Amherst, NY: Prometheus, 2003.
Gregory A. Boyd	*The Myth of a Christian Nation*. Grand Rapids, MI: Zondervan, 2005.
Lenni Brenner, ed.	*Jefferson & Madison on Separation of Church and State: Writings on Religion and Secularism*. Fort Lee, NJ: Barricade, 2005.
Donald L. Drakeman	*Church, State, and Original Intent*. New York: Cambridge University Press, 2010.

Daniel L. Dreisbach — *Thomas Jefferson and the Wall of Separation Between Church and State.* New York: New York University Press, 2002.

Kent Greenawalt — *Religion and the Constitution.* Princeton, NJ: Princeton University Press, 2006.

Isaac Kramnick and R. Laurence Moore — *The Godless Constitution.* New York: Norton, 2005.

Mark Lilla — *The Stillborn God.* New York: Knopf, 2007.

Jon Meacham — *American Gospel.* New York: Random House, 2006.

Mark A. Noll, Nathan O. Hatch, and George M. Marsden — *The Search for Christian America.* Colorado Springs, CO: Helmers & Howard, 1989.

Jonathan A. Wright — *Separation of Church and State.* Santa Barbara, CA: Greenwood, 2010.

Periodicals and Internet Sources

Catherine Ansello — "A Cross to Bear: The Need to Weigh Context in Determining the Constitutionality of Religious Symbols on Public Land," *University of Maryland Law Journal of Race, Religion, Gender and Class*, 2008.

Sandhya Bathija — "A Cross, the Court and the Constitution," *Church & State*, September 2009.

Center for Religion and Public Affairs, Wake Forest University School of Divinity — "Religious Expression in American Public Life: A Joint Statement of Current Law," January 21, 2010. http://divinity.wfu.edu/rpa/.

Christian Century — "Law Puts Cross Under Federal Ownership," September 5, 2006.

Will Connaghan — "What in God's Name Is Happening?" *Daily Record* (St. Louis, MO), December 15, 2006.

Graydon Cox — "America Has a Christian Heritage," *Bucyrus (OH) Telegraph Forum*, June 20, 2009.

John Davis — "Public Holiday Displays Embody Diversity of Faiths," *Poughkeepsie (NY) Journal*, December 16, 2009.

Corey J. Hodges — "Ruling a Victory for Religious Monuments in Parks," *Salt Lake Tribune*, March 6, 2009.

John L. Jackson — "Establishment Clause vs. Memorial Clause," *Chronicle of Higher Education*, October 8, 2009.

Robert Janek — "Questions Abundant in Christianity Debate," *San Angelo (TX) Standard-Times*, March 26, 2009.

Joseph G. Jarret "Law from on High: Religious Displays on Public Property," *Florida Bar Journal*, December 2005.

William S. Jeffrey "Scalia's Cross: The Establishment Clause Does Not Prohibit Religious Memorials," *Harvard Salient*, November 1, 2009.

Kenneth Jost "Courts & The Law: A Way with a Manger," *CQ Weekly*, December 18, 2006.

Liz F. Kay "'Holiday' Trappings: Common Sense Works," *The Sun* (Baltimore, MD), December 17, 2006.

Wendy Koch "Goodwill Lacking in Yule Disputes," *USA Today*, December 21, 2007.

Derek Kravitz "Leesburg Reigns in Its Holiday Display," *Washington Post*, December 1, 2009.

Christopher Levenick "High Noon at Sunrise Rock," *Wall Street Journal*, May 27, 2005.

Michael Lind "America Is Not a Christian Nation," *Salon.com*, April 14, 2009.

Adam Liptak "Religion Largely Absent in Argument About Cross," *New York Times*, October 8, 2009.

Laurel S. Marsh "Myths About the ACLU and Religion," *Prairie Fire*, February 2010.

James M. Mayo and Michael H. Hoeflich — "Commemorating God and Country in American War Memorials: Symbolic Evolution and Legality," *Environment and Behavior*, March 8, 2010.

Jon Meacham — "The End of Christian America," *Newsweek*, April 4, 2009.

Jesse Merriam — "*Salazar v. Buono*: Can Government Give One Religion Prominence in a Public Park?" Pew Forum on Religion & Public Life, September 24, 2009.

Tracie Simer — "Is America Really a Christian Nation?" *Jackson (TN) Sun*, July 4, 2009.

Paul Srubas — "Group Drops Nativity Appeal," *Green Bay (WI) Press-Gazette*, January 15, 2009.

R. Emmett Tyrrell — "The ACLU Talks Too Much," *American Spectator*, July/August 2009.

Weekly Standard — "Cross Enrages," November 9, 2009.

Bill Wineke — "Public Spots Are No Place for Church Symbols," *Wisconsin State Journal*, December 14, 2007.

Index

A

Abrams, Laura, 105
Agnostics, 29, 38, 70
Alito, Samuel A., 19, 76, 89
Alliance Defense Fund (ADF), 100, 106
Amelia Business Association, 105
American Atheists v. Duncan, 82, 84
American Civil Liberties Union (ACLU)
- *County of Allegheny v. ACLU*, 45–46, 92–93, 103
- Hurricane Katrina victims' memorial, 18–20, 22
- *McCreary County v. ACLU of Kentucky*, 10, 23, 48–50, 94–95
- Mojave Desert Veterans Memorial, 32–37, 55–56, 60, 71, 79–80
- Mt. Soledad cross, 65, 70
- Ten Commandment displays, 48

American Civil Rights Union, 64
American Family Association, 106
American Legion, 68
American Principles Project (APP), 60
Americans United (AU), 8–9, 15, 64, 66, 68, 101, 102, 107
Anderson, Bryan J., 40–53
Anti-gay groups, 29
Anti-separationist groups, 66
Appignani Humanist Legal Center, 84–85
Argonne Cross (Arlington National Cemetery), 54–55
Arlington National Cemetery, 54–55
Articles of Confederation (Constitution), 22
Atheists, 22, 29, 37, 38, 66, 70, 82, 84, 101–102

B

Barnard, Brian, 83
Bathija, Sandhya, 62–70, 99–108
Bauer, André, 17
Bazile, Karen Turni, 19
Beezer, Robert R., 67
Berkowitz, Peter, 59
Beshear, Steve, 105
Bill of Rights (Constitution)
- church-state separation in, 27, 30, 84
- displays, 49, 94
- interpretation, 9, 41, 52

Billitteri, Thomas J., 13–17
Black, Hugo, 10
Blackmun, Harry, 46, 47, 104
Bock, Thomas, 68
Brady, Patrick, 71–73
Brennan, William, 46, 47, 91, 92
Brewer, David J., 8
Breyer, Stephen, 19, 84, 96
Buddhism, 37
Burger, Warren, 56, 90–91, 103
Burns, Larry Alan, 65, 67
Bush, George W., 19, 51, 68

C

Camp Smith case, 65
Capitol Square Review and Advisory Board v. Pinette (1995), 42–43
Christ symbology, 44–45, 51, 62, 90, 91, 104
Christianity
 changes with, 11
 Christ symbology, 44–45, 51, 62, 90, 91, 104
 Christmas displays, 28, 59, 72, 83, 87, 100, 105
 cross symbology, 32–33, 54–55, 59, 71–73, 75–76
 "In God We Trust," 15, 17, 25, 42, 55
 other faiths *vs.*, 62–70
 public symbols of, 8, 32–33, 38–39, 59–60
 Ten Commandments displays, 47–48
 See also Church-state separation; Holiday displays; Religious symbols; Ten Commandments
Christmas displays, 28, 59, 72, 83, 87, 100, 105
Church of Holy Trinity v. United States (1892), 8, 41
Church of Jesus Christ of Latter-day Saints, 83
Church-state separation
 barrier to, 10
 in Bill of Rights, 27, 30, 84
 in Constitution, 20–24, 56
 maintaining, 84–85, 89, 107–108
 Religious Right organizations, 102
 as "wall of separation," 10, 23–24, 41
Civic spaces, 31–34
Clinton, Bill, 17
Coercion Test, 43
Cohn, Avern L., 40–53
Constitution (U.S.)
 Articles of Confederation, 22
 church-state separation, 20–24, 56
 free exercise clause, 96
 See also Bill of Rights; Establishment clause; First Amendment
Constitutional Convention, 24–25
Cook, Joe, 19–20
Cooper, Horace, 64–65
Council on American-Islamic Relations, 15
County of Allegheny v. American Civil Liberties Union, Greater Pittsburgh Chapter (1989), 45–46, 92–93, 103, 104
Crèche displays. *See* Nativity scene displays
Crocker, Thomas, 17
Cross symbology, 32–33, 54–55, 59, 71–73, 75–76
 See also Memorial cross displays; Mojave Desert Veterans Memorial; Mt. Soledad cross
Cruz, Ted, 54–57
Currie, Cameron, 17

D

Department of Defense (DoD), 68
Department of Veterans' Affairs, 68, 84
Donohue, Bill, 105–106

E

Eliasberg, Peter, 32–33
Ellis v. City of La Mesa, 67
Endorsement Test, 42–43
Establishment clause (Constitution)
    defined, 84
    in history, 58–61, 92
    interpretation, 41, 52–53, 56, 90–91
    misinterpretation of, 23
    Supreme Court and, 10–11, 25–26, 40, 61
    violation of, 14–15, 36, 44, 88–89, 92–93
    war memorial displays, 32–33, 35–39, 58–61
    See also Religious symbols
Everson v. Board of Education (1947), 9–10, 22–23, 41

F

Falwell, Jerry, 103, 106
Fea, John, 9
First Amendment
    adoption of, 22–23
    government involvement and, 28
    honoring, 20, 102
    ignoring, 81, 85
    misconstruction of, 20–22, 72
    See also Establishment clause; Free exercise clause
Fourteenth amendment (US Constitution), 9
Fraternal Order of Eagles, 50
Free exercise clause (Constitution), 7, 11, 96
Freedom From Religion Foundation, 28, 29
Frum, David, 59
Fugate, Jeff, 105

G

Garnett, Rick, 59
Gaynor, Michael, 18–26
Gerson, Michael, 59
Gillock, Rich, 63
Gingrich, Newt, 78–80
Ginsburg, Ruth Bader, 19, 52, 96
Greenhouse, Linda, 10–11
Gregoire, Christine, 28, 100–101

H

Hadassah organization, 66
Hamodia, 11
Haynes, Charles C., 27–30
Hinduism, 37, 70
Historic memorials, 58–61
Hoft, Jim, 60
Holiday displays
    Christmas displays, 7, 28, 59, 72, 83, 87, 100, 105
    disputes over, 104–106
    in government buildings, 27–30
    laws on, 102–103
    Nativity scenes, 7–8, 16, 45–46, 59, 87–88, 90–92, 100–104
    open public forums over, 101–102
    in public places, 45–46
    Santa Claus displays, 90, 91
    winter solstice, 28, 29, 100–101
Holmes, Oliver Wendell, 90
Holocaust Memorial Museum, 36–37

House Judiciary Committee, 22
Hunter, Duncan, 68
Hurricane Katrina victims' memorial, 18–20, 22
Hutcherson, Ken, 101
Hutson, James, 10
Hyatt, Susan, 106

I

Imperial Grunts (Kaplan), 37
"In God We Trust," 15, 17, 25, 42, 55
Interfaith Alliance, 66
Islam, 16, 37, 70

J

Jefferson, Thomas, 10, 23–24, 27, 30, 41, 84
Jewish War Veterans of the United States of America, 64, 65, 69
Judaism, 16, 32–33, 38, 47, 70, 92, 107
    See also Menorah displays; Star of David symbology

K

Kabbalah Center, 39
Kaplan, Robert D., 37
Katrina, Hurricane, victims' memorial, 18–20, 22
Kellogg, William, 65
Kennedy, Anthony, 46, 47, 59, 76, 92
Khan, Ayesha N., 66
Klazen, Jef, 66
Ku Klux Klan (KKK), 77

L

Lamb's Chapel v. Center Moriches Union Free School District, 43–44
Lemon Test, 42–44, 46, 49–51
Lemon v. Kurtzman, 42
Liberty Counsel, 106
License plate displays, 17
Lincoln, Abraham, 72
Luchenitser, Alex J., 66, 70
Lupu, Ira C., 86–98
Lynch v. Donnelly, 41, 56, 90–92, 103
Lynn, Barry W., 8–9, 15, 16, 107

M

Madison, James, 27, 30
Mansker, Dennis, 64, 101
Marshall, Thurgood, 47, 92
McCreary County v. American Civil Liberties Union of Kentucky (2005), 10, 23, 48–50, 94–95
McLaughlin, Bill, 16
Medved, Michael, 35–39
Memorial cross displays, 18–20, 22, 59–60
Menorah displays, 46–47, 92
Military Association of Atheists and Freethinkers, 66
Military Religious Freedom Foundation, 66
Mojave Desert Veterans Memorial, 32–37, 55–56, 60, 71, 78–80
Moore, E. Ray, Jr., 8
Mormonism, 37
Mt. Soledad cross
    court rulings, 64–66
    ownership of, 67–69

secularizing, 66–67, 69
as Veteran's memorial, 63–64
Murphy v. Bilbray, 67
Muslims, 16, 37, 70

N

National Association of Evangelicals, 15
Native Americans, 24
Nativity scene displays, 7–8, 16, 45–46, 59, 87–88, 90–92, 100–104
Nazism, 77
Neville, Robert C., 33
New America Foundation, 107
New Jersey school board, 9–10
New York Times, 10–11, 107
Noonan, Peggy, 59

O

Obama, Barack, 60
O'Connor, Sandra Day, 42–43, 46, 47, 52, 91, 96
Open public forums, 101–102
O'Reilly, Bill, 28, 99–100
Other faiths, 62–70

P

Patriotic symbols, 71–73
Paulson v. City of San Diego, 67
Peters, Thomas, 60
Pew Forum on Religion & Public Life, 14
Pew Research Center, 14, 87
Phelps, Fred, 29
Pledge of Allegiance, 55
Plessy v. Ferguson, 77
Progressive Christians Uniting, 66
Public land. *See* Religious symbols

R

Racial segregation, 77
Radical secularists, 79
Ramadan, 15
Rasmussen poll, 14
Rehnquist, William, 46, 47, 51, 92, 95–96
Religious Right organizations, 64, 100–102, 105–107
Religious symbols, on public land
allowing, 81–85, 86–98
analysis of, 46–48
approach to, 43–44
banning, 54–57
Christian, 38–39, 44–46
constitutionality of, 87–89
cultural impact, 31–34, 32–34
First Amendment in, 20–22
founder neutrality with, 24–26
freedom, defined, 16
in government space, 27–30
history, 14–15, 22–23
holiday displays, 45–46, 99–108
laws on, 102–103
overview, 13–14, 18–19
permanent installations, 93–97
removing, 35–39
state entanglement, 16–17
as targets, 36–38
tests for, 41–43, 52–53
views on, 15
See also American Civil Liberties Union; Cross symbology; Holiday displays; Mt. Soledad cross; Supreme Court; Ten Commandments; War memorial displays

Ritter, Bob, 81–85
Roberts, John, 19, 76, 89
Rodriguez, Henry "Junior," 19–20
Rodriquez, Gregory, 31–34

S

Salazar vs. Buono, 32, 55, 59, 76–77
Sallman, Warner, 44
Sam, David, 82–83
Santa Claus displays, 90, 91
Satawa, John, 102
Scalia, Antonin
  cross displays, 32
  establishment clause, 11
  Lemon Test, 43–44, 50
  nativity scene displays, 46–47, 92
  Ten Commandment displays, 23, 50, 94–95
Scientology, 39
Secular extremist myth, 21
Secularization, 26, 59, 66–67, 78–80
Senate Judiciary Committee, 21
Separationists, 35–36
Shackelford, Kelly, 54–57
Souter, David, 49, 52, 94, 96
Spinner, Kelly, 16
Star of David symbology, 33, 36–37, 55, 68
State entanglement, 16–17
State ex rel. Finger v. Weedman, 41
Staver, Mat, 106
Stevens, John Paul, 46, 47, 52, 59, 92, 96
Stone, Geoffrey R., 74–77
Stone v. Graham, 47–48, 93–94
Supreme Court (U.S.)
  on constitutional question, 8
  differing opinion within, 89–90
  establishment clause, 10–11, 25–26, 40, 61
  free exercise clause and, 11
  Mojave Desert Veterans Memorial, 55–57, 59–61
  Ten Commandments displays, 10, 14, 47–52
  war memorial displays, 64–66
  See also Religious symbols; individual cases

T

Ten Commandments displays
  debate over, 25, 47–48, 72, 84, 87
  in Kentucky, 10, 14, 23, 48–50, 87, 88, 93–95
  Lemon Test for, 49–51
  in Texas, 10, 48, 50–52, 84, 95–97
Thanksgiving Day proclamation, 51
Thomas, Cal, 103
Thomas More Law Center, 102
Thompson, Gordon, 67
Thompson, Richard, 102
Timlin, Robert J., 55
Treaty of Tripoli, 9
The Truth of Broken Symbols (Neville), 33
Tuttle, Robert W., 86–98

U

Unitarian Universalist Association, 66

Utah Highway Patrol Association, 69, 82

V

Van Orden v. Perry, 10, 48, 50–52, 84, 95–97
Veterans' Memorial, 63–64
Veterans of Foreign Wars (VFW), 36, 76, 79–80
Vidal v. Girard's Executors, 41
Virginia Bill for Religious Liberty, 23
Virginia Statute of Religious Freedom, 24

W

"Wall of separation," 10, 23–24, 41
War memorial displays
 attacks on, 32–33, 78–80
 court rulings on, 64–66
 establishment clause, 32–33, 35–39, 58–61
 other faiths and, 62–70
 as patriotic symbols, 71–73
 as religious symbols, 35–39, 74–77
Washegesic v. Bloomingdale Public Schools, 44
Washington, George, 9, 24, 51
Washington Department of General Administration, 101
The Washington Times, 64, 100
White, Byron, 46, 47, 92
Wiccans, 37, 68, 70
Wildmon, Donald, 106
Williams, David, 105
Winter solstice displays, 28, 29, 100–101
Winters, Michael Sean, 58–61
Witherspoon, John, 61

Z

Zweiman, Bob, 63–64